Instinctive
Fly Fishing

Instinctive
Fly Fishing

A Guide's Guide to Better Fishing

TAYLOR STREIT

THE LYONS PRESS
GUILFORD, CONNECTICUT

An imprint of The Globe Pequot Press

The Lyons Press is an imprint of The Globe Pequot Press.

10 9 8 7 6 5 4 3 2

Printed in the United States of America

Designed by Sterling Hill Productions

Library of Congress Cataloging-in-Publication Data

Streit, Taylor.
  Instinctive fly fishing : a guide's guide to the basics of fly fishing / Taylor Streit.
      p. cm.
Includes bibliographical references (p.   ) and index.
  ISBN 1-59228-190-7 (HC : alk. paper)
  1. Fly fishing. 2. Fly fishing—Guidebooks. I. Title.
SH456.S84 2004
799.12'4--dc22
                                        2003017225

For Chelsea, Mom, and Sandra

Contents

Acknowledgments

On looking back over a lifetime of fly fishing, I realize that many fine fishermen and writers helped make this book. The first of these was, quite appropriately, my dad, the late Phil Streit, who plopped me on the bank of a stream in New York fifty years ago. Then, when I was a kid on foot, Mike Lucas, Bill Luty, Herb Dickerson, and Pat Keating all found time to take me fishing. Special thanks to Fran Betters for officially getting me started in the fly-fishing business in my teens.

After moving to New Mexico I was tutored by Bill Vickers, Charlie Reynolds, and Mike Wiley. In later years, I have learned a lot from New Mexicans Chris Jarvis, Justin Spence, Garrett VeneKlasen, Keith Loveless, and Bob Widgren.

Heavy Rolle and Felix Smith of South Andros, Bahamas, taught me tricks with their "trow lines." Argentines Lorenzo Sympson, Pedro Arencet, and Arturo Dominguez have added to my education.

And I have learned a lot from many outstanding fishermen that I have guided—too many to name, but Dale White Sr. and Shane Mills come to mind.

And many thanks to that famous Colorado angler, my brother Jackson Streit, who has contributed much to this book.

Many fine writers have helped me along with this project, including Tracy McCallum, Nick Lyons, John Nichols, Tom Taylor, John Judy, and Dan Boyne.

Thanks to Mary Lou Palaski for watching the kids, and the fly shop while I was out guiding and doing "research."

Last, but not least, is my son Nick, who helped immensely with many aspects of this book. I may have taught him to fish, but he has gone way past what I gave him to become an incredible guide in his own right.

Introduction

Long before I was a fishing guide I was a fly fisherman. Much of what I knew about the sport—or thought I knew—came from reading and other fly fishers. When the "sport" turned into a profession, I discovered that there is a big difference between being a casual fisherman and having to feed your family by fishing. Most of my faintly conceived notions couldn't stand up against the naked truth of experience. Now, after a quarter century of guiding, my perceptions about catching trout are based on personal experience.

Those 25 years of guiding have shown me that the keys to fly-fishing success are usually just common-sense rules of Mother Nature: keep the sun at your back and your fly in the water; and think like a predator. Such observations are rather mundane details, and that makes them unpopular with complicated fly-fishing types. We fly fishers revel in complexity and choose convoluted solutions over simple ones.

This has a lot to do with our times. When I started fly fishing, folks were more connected with the natural world than they are now. It was a more rural land then, and people spent more time outdoors. Many were already hunters and fishermen, and taking up fly fishing was just part of a natural progression that started with bait fishing and went on to spinners before graduating to the fly rod. They learned a lot about trout and the ways of Mother Nature along the way.

The new millennium finds most of us are strangers in the natural world. With everything computerized, categorized, and virtualized, the modern fly fisher has developed an overly tech-

The author with a monster brown trout. Instincts and common sense play big roles in becoming a good fisherman. Credit: Bill Rector

nical and analytical approach to the sport. His leaders need to be constructed with micrometers; the thorax of his fly needs to be tied out of opossum—not common 'possum, mind you, but the rare Siberian Opossum. Overburdened with all these theories, formulas, and flies he splashes ungracefully into the stream. Dragging all that stuff along can be more of a burden than an asset. Knowledge and gear don't, in themselves, make a fisherman, and they are poor substitutes for simply knowing how to fish.

Defining "how to fish" is elusive. You can't see it, taste it, or smell it, but we all know that some people know how to fish a heck of a lot better than others. The problem is that many of the things that make a great fisherman are things that he does instinctively and subconsciously. Ask him why he ducked there or chose to fish a pool from that particular spot, and he wouldn't know.

A few years ago, I tried to get this idea down on paper. I sat and typed at the computer, but what came out sounded too much like most of what I had been reading all my life. I finally realized that much of what I was trying to capture was intuitive, predatory skills too slippery to be so easily caught and written down. I concluded that the only place to get in touch with this primal fisherman was on the water. So, over a period of several years I yapped into a little tape recorder. I kept notes on both stream and lake, in New Mexico, Colorado, and Argentina, with clients who represented every phase of the learning curve.

The tapes revealed that the modern fly fisher's instincts are indeed hidden deep in the forest—on the back branches of his family tree—and that on the trout stream common sense "ain't very common." In between all the screw-ups and blunders, tangled lines and hooked thumbs, a lot of fish *were* caught, however, and I paid careful attention to the often-subtle reasons why those fish took the fly. I found that there were a thousand factors that helped catch those fish, many of which I had never noticed in all my years of guiding. What follows are those thousand things.

Chapter 1

INSTINCTIVE FLY FISHING

"If industrial man continues to multiply his numbers and expand his operations he will succeed in his apparent intention, to seal himself off from the natural and isolate himself within a synthetic prison of his own making."

—Edward Abbey, *Desert Solitaire*

The osprey dangles above the water on beating wings—intense eyes fixed on its prey. Every atom in its body has but one goal: Catch the fish. It doesn't chat with itself while this is going on: "Perhaps I should go around the next bend; this trout is too deep." The animal instinctively knows those answers. A decision is made from somewhere deep inside. The fluttering wings become rigid, and the bird whirls and plunges. When the water explodes above the trout, the startled creature has but a wisp of time to flee. The fish that ponders will be eaten.

The human fisherman doesn't have—or *have* to have—a fraction of that concentration. He's just standing there in midstream, mouth ajar, staring into his fly box. At times he may actually *be* fishing, but he's as likely to be puttering around the edges of it rather than actually *doing* it. "Should I try that pool up there?" he asks himself. "Maybe with a different fly? Didn't I read that—oh, was that a splash? Did I just have a strike? Where was I?"

Few of us ever get to the gifted state that is all action, and if and when we do reach that blissful place where instincts guide movements, it usually can be captured only fleetingly. Michael

The instinctive fly fisherman may not stand out in a crowd—but you'll know one when you see one. Credit: Peter Lloyd

Jordan's "zone," the music in Mozart's ear—that God-given state of perfection—is unobtainable to those who are constantly supposing, thinking, and changing flies. Certainly, the intellectual will sink a basket here and there, but the real pro knows that when it is time to play, instincts rule the game.

It is on rare occasions that you will spot this instinctive fisherman on the water. He doesn't stand out, and your eyes would more likely be drawn to the person midstream winging a long line. To the untrained eye the long caster is the one who looks the part, while the real expert may not draw much attention. He's slinking along the bank, dangling a few feet of line in carefully chosen spots. His movements are those of an animal on the prowl rather than of an urban technician.

His attitude is positive and isn't hampered with the second guesses that shame most anglers out of the action. It isn't a bubbly "top of the morning to you" attitude, just a confidence that says, "A fish is going to eat my fly any second!" This guy may have little faith in life, other people, and himself. Maybe that is why he fishes so much. His positivity makes him all eyes, all ears, all present and accounted for.

Another phenomenon that I have observed is called, for lack of a better word, luck. That's what we call it, but that isn't exactly what it is. Put two guys of seemingly equal talent on the water, and one will almost always outfish the other. I see this all the time when guiding: The one guy who you assume will catch a lot of fish doesn't. This fellow often *talks* a good game but may have no *feel* for the outdoors. His ability to not catch fish is astounding, and he does the wrong thing at just the right time. He will take the fly out of the water just as a trout is rising to eat it. I'll jump a foot in the air and say, "Didn't you see that fish?"

"No," he says. The guy wades up a stream like a grizzly chasing salmon, and when he finally hooks a fish he fights it with equal delicacy.

The other guy, the one who catches the fish, has a common-sense nature that is responsive to instructions from the guide, the stream, and the fish. He may not even know many of the details of the sport, but they are the easy part. They can be learned.

Although no easy matter, the instinctive, the intuitive can be learned, and you can become "lucky" too. I have guided many people who were at first out of place on the water, but I've found that if they stick with it, they start fitting in, to eventually become good, natural fly fishers.

How does the modern fly fisherman get schooling in Mother Nature's ways? First, you must eliminate that which interferes with your *focused* pursuit of fish. This may mean as little as cleaning up your fishing vest of all unnecessary items or as much as cleaning up your way of life. Maybe it's your stressful job, cranky spouse, or boisterous kids that are keeping you distracted and out of the water. If any of these factors get in the way of your fly fishing, they gotta go! I know some of you will hem and haw on this point, so for those who are not willing to go to *any* lengths, here are some watered-down suggestions—compromises, if you will— that should help bring more cohesion between human and fish.

Do things that get you in touch with your natural self: meditate, smell flowers, get off that choppy hip/hop and listen to something that flows, like Vivaldi or Coltrane. And go fishing, of course. I don't mean fly fishing. Get yourself a cane pole, some stink bait, and a bobber and head to the catfish hole. Don't scoff at the idea of bait fishing; there's a lot to be learned from it. Bait fishing offers one thing that fly fishing lacks—foreplay. There's a heavenly period when you are letting the fish eat the bait, which doesn't happen when fishing with most artificials. The rod is tapping, the line is tugging, and you become filled with anticipation because you know the throbbing rod comes next!

When your catfish is safely ashore, whack it on the head and then yank the skin off with pliers. If you get your hands covered with guts and stuck by catfish spikes, so much the better. While lounging on the bank after you have barbecued your fish be sure

Why do fish like this start biting at certain times? Why do they stop? Truly observant anglers often know.

to watch the wind shake the leaves on the trees and notice how the clouds grow and drift. Take your shoes off, stand in the mud along the bank, and let it ooze up between your toes. Whatever you do, don't—I repeat don't—take along any reading about the life cycle of aquatic insects. Suggested reading could include "Big Two-Hearted River," by Hemingway, or the works of Roderick Haig-Brown.

Haig-Brown writes with beautiful skill and with the simplicity of someone who has mastered his craft. He spent his life out-doors and sees beyond the frivolous details to the basic elements: water and weather conditions, amount of fishing pressure, timing and attitude. In *A River Never Sleeps*, he writes about a difficult fish: "...they always like it; they aren't chalk-stream fish or even fish that live near a city; they'll come if it looks like food." He made that comment when faced with a fish that wouldn't take the fly that he always used at that place and circumstance. He ultimately did have to change flies and tactics to catch the fish, but he wisely started out with the premise that the fish were dumb. That way he could just go along catching them with a tried and true method and fly until he ran into a tough fish. He didn't get to the water and invent problems and complications; he simply fished and dealt with a situation when it arose.

He writes that he didn't catch any large fish on a particular day because the water was warm. End of story. He didn't wrack his brain about this. It is simply a fact that larger trout don't feed well in warmish water. All the fly changing in the world won't alter that. Certain things may work better than others under those circumstances, but if the angler remembers the elementary fact about water temperature, he will make better decisions about where and how to fish.

And fish just don't eat all the time. All species of fish are subject to this rule, and all species of fisherman, especially fly fishermen, are reluctant to accept this. When faced with the dilemma, a fly fisherman will change flies and fish harder rather than taking a nap or watching the river flow—something to get him rested so that when the fish do start feeding, the angler will be fresh and ready. You'll probably learn a lot more from your observation post than you would by beating the water to a froth. Like *why* and *when* the fish start biting. Usually there is a subtle change of weather that turns the fish—or insects—on.

Plan your next trip away from the popular tailwaters. Shoulder-to-shoulder fishing for big trout brings out the worst in many anglers. I find myself cramming my lunch down my throat while cursing at the guy across the river who has the audacity to catch more fish than me. Fishing smaller, more remote streams with spooky little trout will develop your predatory instincts. There you will discover that keeping the sun at your back, and staying low and in the shade are really important. The skills you pick up will be of benefit in many other fishing situations.

Another helpful pursuit that has fallen out of favor in some circles is hunting— quiet steps in the shadows, crawling, and slipping between trees. It demands all of one's senses and intelligence. When fresh sign is spotted, instincts as old as time arise, the nostrils open, ears and eyes strain, and the clutter in the mind clears. The human animal is again in his natural place.

Most helpful is being observant on the water. You'll absorb a lot more information than you might realize that will later spill out as intuition. Some day you'll be able to just stick your head out the door and sense if the fish are biting: Your nose will catch the scent of the still, moist air that trout love; your eyes will notice that the light is slanted about right; and before you know it, you'll be on your way to the river wondering how the fly rod found its way into your hand.

Chapter Two

THE FLY-FISHING PERSONALITY

Spending the day with folks engaged in the intense game of fly fishing will teach you a lot about people. After years of observing my fellow fisherman I feel like an amateur psychologist ready to pontificate on the subject of the "fly-fishing personality." Following are several that I have identified.

The author and his son Nick, also an established fishing guide. Between them, they have seen all types of fishermen. Credit: Justin Spence

Analytical Fly Fisherman

The analytical fly fisherman keeps so busy fiddling with his formulas, strategies, and entomological charts that the simple, straightforward solutions to catching a fish are often overlooked. If, for instance, he can't catch a fish, he should examine the obvious first: Has the fish actually seen the fly? Has the fish seen him? Heck, maybe the fish can't even see. I once approached a client who was casting to a dead trout lying on the bottom of the river. He told me that it wouldn't "take" and was showing the decomposing animal a new fly as I arrived. To first study the condition of such a docile creature might have been the common-sense thing to do, but as a cabby once told me, "Common sense ain't common."

The Jiggler

The jiggler is a stressed-out breed of angler commonly found residing in large cities. Far removed from his ancestral homeland his senses get overloaded when near trout water. And when approaching said water his body vibrates as if it were electrically charged, thereby oscillating the fly rod to form a tangled ball of line, leader, and fly. Although cardiac problems are a possibility, there are more practical concerns: This angler's fly seldom sits still long enough to catch a fish. The jiggler also changes flies often, always thinking that the next fly will be *the one*. With those shaky fingers, however, it is a time-consuming process and should be avoided.

If the jiggler should somehow hook a good fish, the chances are slim that it will be landed. If a person is that excitable *before* a trout is actually hooked, imagine what happens when he latches onto one. The hyper angler hates to give a fish line and can generally be counted on to freeze hysterically when a big fish takes, breaking the leader and losing the treasure.

The jiggler will invariably generate unnecessary tension in the casting arm, and that rigidity takes the feel out of the casting operation. Because he cannot feel the line loading, the timing of the cast becomes a guessing game. His uncertainty tends to make him perform many needless false casts.

The Lazy Angler

The lazy angler doesn't take care of his fly and slack line, causing him to get bad drifts and missed strikes. He is not prudent about slack line, and it gets tangled with rocks, brush, and his appendages. This keeps the fly out of the water—and the fish's mouth.

I remember a client who complained about the day's fishing. He didn't have any right to because he fished with one hand in his pocket all day. Fly fishing in streams, if done correctly, is a lot of work. Pick up all the slack line, try that difficult cast under the brush, wade that extra step or see what's up that channel you've never fished. Save lazy for the catfish hole.

The Overeager Angler

The opposite, the overeager anglers, are folks who get so obsessed that they pound the water like lunatics. When you find yourself doing this, listen to the little gurgling noises, take deep breaths, and remember that it's only fishing. Thinking there just might be a nice fish behind every rock, this angler tends to fish every inch of water in sight. All really good fishermen have a no-doubt outlook, believing that each cast is going to catch a fish, but that attitude needs to be tempered with good judgment, or there will be a lot of wasted effort.

Such overeager anglers start pulling line out for the next cast while they are fishing the present one. (This type of angler feels it is necessary to always make a longer cast.) This is sloppy and distracts from fishing the cast that is on the water. If you are a good hand with the rod, you may be able to pull line out of the reel at the same time as you are fishing. But no matter who you are, you'll catch more fish if you do one thing at a time.

Fired-Up Fly Fisher

This fired-up fly fisher is so dedicated that he gets worn out before the dance starts. No matter what your mind says, the body has only so much juice in it, so plan your time wisely. For instance, the long evenings of early summer can provide the best hatches and fishing of the season, so I often try to convince wound-up clients that we shouldn't start early in the morning. Not wanting to appear to be a slacker, however, I seldom push it. Invariably, this person tires and will want to quit around sundown, just when things will start to happen, or they will be so pooped by then that they end up doing a sloppy job and missing all the strikes.

The Materialistic Fisherman

We all like to catch big fish, but for many that is the only criterion used to judge the quality of the day. Materialistic fishermen are so focused on achieving their goal that they seldom see a hawk fly by or hear the wind rustling the trees. All they care about is results—and that means big fish, period! This keeps them out of some wonderful places that don't happen to have those fish. Such myopic anglers would actually catch more fish if they got more attuned to the world around them.

The Drifter

Another common and amusing sort of fly fisher is known as the Drifter. You can take him from town to country, but his mind seldom accompanies him. This makes him, of course, unaware of what is happening around him.

Bob is a good case in point. I was having a heck of a time trying to teach Chicago Bob to cast. Bob was one of those laugh-a-minute cats who is always looking for a joke—even if it is at his expense—so I'm sure that he wouldn't mind me telling you this little tale. (He may have even planned the whole thing.)

We were in the middle of a stream where I was trying to teach Bob to cast and fish. He seemed to have finally gotten somewhat of a loose grip on the casting operation, so I went off to check on his partner. I returned a short while later to see if he had had any luck. As I walked across a meadow I could see Bob in the distance making some very puzzling motions with his fly rod. Bob's casting had deteriorated beyond my expectations, which were not high. His line was traveling in wide, circular loops, and his arm had to go round and round like a windmill to maintain this sort of lasso effect. Getting closer, I was able to analyze the problem and called out.

"Hey Bob, there is a fish on your line." When I reached Bob he told me that he had been having difficulty with his casting for some time. The very dead look of the four-inch trout supported the idea that the fish had been attached for some time.

The Open-Minded Angler
The open-minded angler uses the experience and expertise acquired on his home water elsewhere, but is not a slave to it. All trout streams are different, and if you step into new water with a lot of preconceived notions, you may go fishless. A good example of this is when a tailwater fisherman fishes a new trout stream. Because he is used to being surrounded by both fish and fishermen he is programmed to move at a slow pace. This is inappropriate for a normal trout stream because a regular freestone stream doesn't hold as many fish as a tailwater. The trout, less pressured in the freestone stream, might take a fly the first time it goes over their head. Consequently covering lightly fished water quickly is wise.

This open-minded angler pays attention to what is going on around him and goes at a relaxed enough pace that he can absorb the subtle hints that nature constantly supplies to the observant. This person also solicits help and advice from others and is willing to learn new things.

In general, however, fishermen have sensitive egos, so, as with the rest of the human race, open-mindedness is not common. Who ever heard an angler blame himself for a poor day's fishing? "I was off my game." No, that quote is for sports that don't have

Are you an open-minded fisherman? Lazy? Over-eager? Personality makes a difference when fishing.

so many built-in excuses. Fishermen have been graciously excluded from personal responsibility ever since the first one of our kind stooped through the cave door with an empty stringer and stuttered, "They aren't biting." We fly fishers are above such common lies and have developed a plethora of elaborate excuses appropriate to our lofty position in the hierarchy of fishing. "I didn't have any No. 26s," "My leader wasn't fluorocarbon," and "My guide sucked," are just a few.

Do you identify with any of these personality disorders? Rehabilitation is possible if you are ready to put the responsibility where it belongs—on yourself. If we do that, we will become better fishermen.

Chapter Three

TIPS

Here is a potpourri of tips I have gathered from my fly-fishing and guiding experience. Hopefully, they can help you catch more fish and increase the enjoyment of the outing.

Use Wide-Gap Hooks

I have kept score on the hookup percentages and found that flies tied on hooks with narrow gaps do not hook and hold fish well. Flies tied on them should be avoided. Wide-gap hooks catch more fish!

Keep Hooks Sharp

If you miss several fish, check your fly's sharpness by running the hook point against your fingernail at a sharp angle. If it digs in, it's sharp; if it slides, it needs sharpening. If you don't have a hook sharpener, pick up one of those smooth rocks at your feet and hone the point with it.

Walking Pays Off

We do a lot of walking in Argentina and the southern Rockies where I fish and guide. I prefer to fish water that hasn't been hammered, and, for my money, with each mile walked and each hill climbed, the quality of both the fishing and the experience rises dramatically. I like getting the walking over with at the beginning of the day if possible. This usually means hiking down-river and then fishing back up. I try to time this so that I start fishing when I expect the fish to start biting. I have found it wise to

Sharp hooks make a difference on tough-jawed old fish like this.

not rig the rod until I have reached my planned destination. If I have it rigged, it's getting stuck in the brush all the time. Besides, I can't help but put casts here and there as I go; that's a half-assed way to fish.

Instead, this is the time to scout: Check out the water and look for insects and indications that will clue you in on how to fish. When ready to choose a fly and style of fishing, I try to listen to my instincts. They may have learned more on the walk than I consciously realized.

Point Your Rod Forward

When strolling, crawling, and swearing your way through brush keep your rod pointed in front of you. This gives you more control, allowing you to aim it where you would like. And if you do get it stuck, you don't have to go back to where you've already been to set the fly free. When going through very thick brush, raise your arm and point the rod straight up.

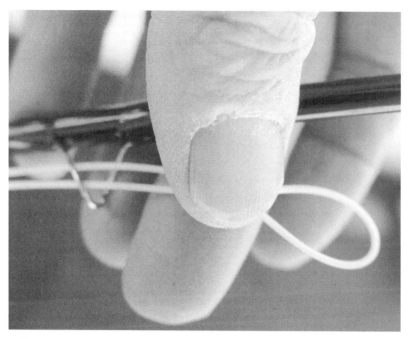

Fold the fly line into a loop when stringing up the rod. Credit: Wes Edling

Easy Way to Thread Your Leader

Rather than trying to finagle an invisible and slippery leader end through the guides, fold the fly line over double and run it through the guides. It is more manageable and if it escapes from your fingers, it won't scamper back down the rod like a leader will.

When the End of the Leader Goes Below the Tiptop

When the fly line gets sucked into the rod you don't have to always go through the hassle of reaching for the end of the rod and pulling it out manually. Put the fly in the current and pull it against the flow a couple of times, and it will usually get the fly line back out of the guides. Some outfits are more prone to this nuisance than others. Using too long a leader in short-line situations exacerbates this problem.

Go with the Flow

Don't get frustrated by trying to catch your fly in the wind. Point the rod into the blow and let it come to you.

Forget Something?

Ever find that you have forgotten something when you reach the stream? Of course you have. Then try the "pat down." Start by patting your head: "Yes, I have a hat on." Continue down the body by checking for the appropriate gear for that section, finishing the body count with: "Yes, I have my shoes on." Close your eyes and make a pretend cast; then mentally picture all the gear you need for that: flies, leaders, rod, reel, line, and anything else. Ask yourself what you need should you hook a fish, and so on.

Keep Your Fly Clean

Cleaning debris from flies can be time consuming, especially when you are nymph fishing in mossy streams. You usually won't have to manually remove moss from a fly if you learn this little trick. Make a very a short and wicked cast that snaps the fly right at the surface. When you make the cast, think of cracking a whip, so that the end of the whip—your fly—hits the water at the speed of sound. If done properly, this type of cast will clean the moss off the fly most of the time. If you are fishing with a lot of weight and have to sling the fly around in an oval, modify the slap. Just as the fly meets the surface rip it back as fast as you can. Of course, cast away from where you are fishing, so as not to alarm the quarry.

Less Knots the Better

Since knots are the weakest link in the chain, and tying them cuts down on actual fishing time, reducing their number is a good idea. When you are tying on tippet to fish a multiple-fly setup, use one piece of tippet for the job. When you tie on the fly closest to you (the hand fly) simply leave the tag end of your Clinch Knot the desired length for the tail fly. You don't need to make an Improved Clinch Knot, just a Clinch, because the tag can't slip when it is that long. When fishing multiple wet flies that are going to be retrieved, tie the additional flies to the bend of the hook so that they swim straight.

Instant Beadhead Fly

Need to get down deeper or need an instant beadhead fly? Carry beads with you and slip one on your leader in front of the fly. This works with small beads, but large beads can cut the leader. To minimize that possibility, turn the bead around so that the concave end faces you.

Durable Flies

Tired of flies falling apart? Here is a tip I learned from international angler Garrett VeneKlasen while fishing with him for peacock bass in the Amazon. Tie your flies with Super Glue instead of head cement. If you don't tie the flies you fish, put a tiny drop behind the heads of those you use. They will last forever.

Fly-Box Insurance

If you've never lost a box of flies, you will. My client, Mark Yarbrough, puts his name and phone number on all his fly boxes and then waterproofs his labeling with a covering of transparent tape. (Offering a reward for their return is another option.)

Keep Your Socks Clean

To avoid getting your socks covered with earthen materials when changing in and out of your waders, keep a little piece of carpet (or floor mat from the vehicle) to stand on when you change in and out of your gear.

Cars and Rods

I have had fly rods broken by all sorts of critters, but the nastiest varmint is the automobile. So when gearing up to fish, take your rod out of the vehicle last. Reverse the order at the end of the day, putting the rod away first. Never lean rods in the convenient wedge made by an open door. Leaning a rod against the side of the car is a bad idea too, because it has no purchase and can slide. If you must have a rigged rod near the auto, lean it against trees a few feet away from the action. Don't forget that it's there. Finally, don't put your rod on top of your car, for it is easy to drive off and forget it, as I've done twice!

Dry-Fly Resuscitation

When your hackled dry flies get crushed and matted, you can restore them with steam. Hold the fly with forceps or pliers over the steam vented from a boiling teakettle, and watch the hackles spring to life before your very eyes!

Glare Remover

Every fisherman should wear polarized sunglasses for more productive fishing, safer wading, and increased eye comfort. Tan is the best all-round shade.

Leave Your White Hat at Home

Avoid wearing white hats when fishing over spooky fish. White stands out more than any other color.

No Butts About It

Get rid of the butt section of your leader. The average angler will cast much better without it because a tapered leader is designed to be used as is, and the addition of a "butt section" will hinder performance.

Keep It Simple

I see a lot of different knots, loops, and gizmos at the ends of fly lines, but I have found that loops get tangled, braided connections pull out, and gizmos corrode. When clients have those complicated couplings I beg them to let me reduce the mess to one simple knot: a Uni Knot. The Uni is not as smooth a connection as the Nail Knot, but you can tie it quickly.

Prevent Tangles

When you take your outfits for a car or boat ride, they behave well at first, but they eventually get tangled in cramped quarters. And by the time you reach your destination they are all enmeshed. My brother, Jackson Streit, showed me how to keep the rascals under control.

First, be sure the fly is secured in the keeper or impaled in the cork handle, with the line just barely snug. Next, grasp the line outside the rod about halfway up the rod and wrap it around the rod three times. Finally, take the line that is coming out of the reel and wrap it around the back of the reel. (It is necessary to take a little line out of the reel to do this.) This will keep the line snug against the rod, where it can't get into trouble.

Take the Wind Out of Your Knots

Check for wind knots often. Remember that they reduce the strength of your leader by 50 percent and should never be allowed to remain. If wind knots are detected early, they can be opened with a hook point; even better, use two hook points, one in each hand, and get them in the knot. If you can't open and untie the knot, cut the leader and start over.

Reel Handy Advice

I recommend setting up the reel so that you wind with your master hand. You do have to switch hands to get a fish on the reel, but

Reeling with your primary hand gives you an edge—plus, holding the rod in your other hand frees your master hand for netting and landing.

you get used to that in no time, and you can reel much more adeptly with your primary hand. This is important when you are fighting a fish that swims at you, because hooks often fall out when tension is lost. Trout don't usually swim very fast, but when a bonefish charges you, you have to reel very fast in order to take up the slack. This setup also frees your primary hand to actually land the fish.

Dealing with Tangles

Master guide John Judy of Sisters, Oregon, pointed out to me that when people reel line with the nondominant hand the rod wobbles, causing tangles around the rod tip. If the tangle is at the end of the rod, lower it as gingerly as possible so that nothing gets jostled on the way down. If you aren't careful, another tangle can form when a loop of line from the middle of the rod swings around and around the rod. Look along the rod at the tangle before you do anything with it; you may find that you can flip the middle section of the mess back around the rod the way it came. Reel smoothly and watch the rod when you reel if you have a tendency to get this sort of tangle. If a beadhead fly gets tangled around the end of the rod, don't jiggle it. One good jiggle will send it around the rod a dozen times.

When a tangle occurs at the top end of a long fly rod, it is, of course, necessary to get the mess in front of you so that you can straighten it out. If you are on the bank, you can just put the reel down to get at the snarl. If you are in the middle of the river, don't be afraid to put the reel into the water. I see clients going through all sorts of contortions to keep their reel dry. It's only water, and it is actually a good idea to dunk your reel now and then to get the sand out of it. Of course, keep all gear out of salt water and be sure to keep reels with cork drags dry.

Tangles form very subtly in your reel over time. When you wind your leader all the way into your reel, that end worms its way under other coils of line. The next time you pull line out of the reel, this loop slides down the fly-line to later lodge in the backing. If you fish a lot, this happens over and over and you can have quite a mess brewing down there. This is easily averted if you simply *don't reel the line in all the way*. Leave a few inches of leader sticking out of the reel.

Another common tangle appears when a loop of line crosses over the rod between two consecutive eyes. To fix this little and common problem, slip that section of line over the end of the rod and then bring the fly through the loop.

Don't Walk and Fish Simultaneously

I'm often guilty of this, and I imagine I've missed a few thousand trout because of it. When you finish fishing a spot, stop to examine the water ahead for the next attractive fishing location and, just as important, for the best place from which to fish it. Remember that your first cast into a spot is the one most likely to get a hit, but if the cast is made before you get into proper

When a loop of line crosses over the rod between two eyes, slip that section of line over the rod tip and pull through.

position, the fly may drag over the fish and spook it. And don't fish while you're moving. It's sloppy business, and you won't be ready if you get a strike and the motions of casting and wading simultaneously send alarming wakes.

Thumbs Up for the Proper Hold

Some anglers have the bad habit of holding and casting the fly rod with the index finger, rather than the thumb, on top of the handle. They initially learned to do this—for an honorable enough reason—as it was hard to break their wrist if their index finger was on top. But when a really powerful cast is needed, the index finger can't provide enough strength for the job.

Finger Food for Thought

Many anglers, including some very good ones, use the index finger to pick up line. That is the finger that we naturally use for such work, but since the finger supports the rod, the grip is

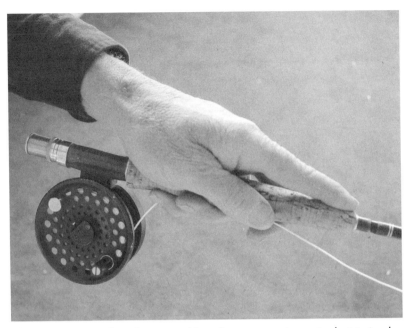

This position may be okay in making short, accurate casts, but is inadequate for longer throws. Credit: Wes Edling.

Proper hand position with thumb up and line under middle finger. Credit: Wes Edling.

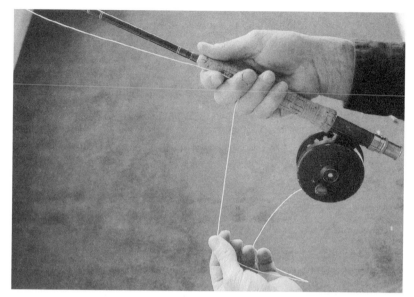

Your hands should be in this position when taking up slack line.

sometimes compromised when using it. Although it may take some time getting used to, the middle finger will do a better job. It is easier to find the line with the longer appendage and the hand's position on the handle is not altered when reaching for the line.

Taking Up the Slack

A common fault of inexperienced fly fishers in picking up slack—and playing fish—is reaching above the "pickup finger" to grab the line. This wastes a lot of effort, because the line needs to be repositioned under the pickup finger after each stroke. Strikes are missed because the line is taken up in awkward little jerks, and, half the time, the fingers are out of position to set the hook. When you grab the line from below the pickup finger, you are always ready to set the hook. Just clamp down on the line with the middle finger and drive the steel home.

By approaching this still pool from the side—with the sun behind him—this angler has fooled a nice trout.

Heads or Tails

In smaller streams you may *not* want to approach long, still pools from below. The fish in the shallow water at the tail of the pool are usually smaller trout. But if alarmed they will run upstream and alert their larger neighbors. So instead of spooking the whole pool, take to the bank well below the pool, slip around and approach the head of the pool from the side. The bigger trout will most likely be there, and because the water will be deeper and broken, you will be less visible to the fish.

Rocky Lies

Feeding trout very often sit in the cushion right in front of big rocks. When a submerged fly gets close to a boulder, most anglers whip it to the surface well upstream of the spot and miss a good opportunity. Let the fly get very close to the rock and then, by lifting the rod slowly, ease the fly out of the water right in front of the boulder. That way the trout will have a chance to catch it.

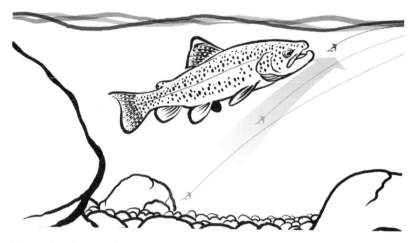

Don't whip flies to the surface at end of drift—let this guy catch one.

Wading Shoe Savvy

Frozen wading shoes, or old ones that have become very dry, are tough to put on in the morning. If the temperatures are expected to dip below freezing overnight, take your wet shoes inside. If you have old ratty leather wading shoes, soak them before you try putting them on.

Net Attachments

I have tried a bunch of different means of attaching my net to my vest, and I have come to the conclusion that the French snap is still the best. I have lost nets in brush with the magnet attachments, and I've tried other devices. The only problem with the French snap is that you have to reach behind yourself to unhook it.

When you are fighting a big fish you don't want to use the net until the fish is worn out. That's the time to reach for the net.

Blackened Trout

We normally release trout, but occasionally it can be good for a stream to keep them. For instance, in some little streams the trout are so small and numerous that culling will give the larger fish room to grow. If you decide to keep some of these smaller fish and want to munch some on the stream, but don't have any cooking gear handy, try my "blackened trout" recipe. (The modern catch-and-release fly fisher may not have much experience killing a trout. Hold it near the tail and whack its head on a rock to dispatch it.)

Impale one gutted 8-inch trout with a green willow stick inserted in its mouth. Place it onto a roaring fire; "roaring" is the key word here. Don't wait for coals to form. Remove the trout before the willow stick burns up—about 3 minutes. You will know the trout is done when the fins are burned off and the fish has been sufficiently "blackened." Add lemon and salt if you have them available.

Hot and Cold Advice

Cold winter and hot summer conditions present challenges and solutions.

For example, excellent fly fisher Justin Spence taught me that when I'm fishing in the winter, I should spray aerosol cooking oil on my rod's guides to keep them from icing up.

When it's hot, try cleaning your eyeglasses in soapy water before you fish, and they won't fog up. When fishing in salt water, carry a clean hand towel in a sealed bag to clean sun-glasses. Stay cool by keeping a wet towel around your head. In very hot weather, wear absorbent clothes—and take a dip every now and then.

I put sunblock on a couple of times a day. I also wear long sleeves and sun gloves. Don't put sunblock on your forehead, because if you sweat it runs into your eyes. I burn on my neck and chest. Be wise and goop on there, too.

The Happy De-Hooker

I have seen a lot of humans hooked, and I have noticed that get-ting impaled isn't as bad as staying impaled. It's wearing the fly

When the victim is hooked with a large fly, a loop of mono or other heavy line will allow you to pull the hook straight back.

that seems to bother people. Whether a doctor or a fisherman removes the fly, it has to come out, and the operation might as well be performed sooner rather than later.

I would like to share with you a system of unhooking people that I have used over the years. The first step is to cut the leader above the fly. As I'm doing this, I start the psychological phase of the operation by explaining the options: "We could leave this great fishing spot and go to the emergency room." That aims the patient's thinking in the right direction. Next I explain a gruesome method of hook removal that we are not going to use: "We could run it all the way through, cut the point off with pliers, and then back it out." That description gets the patient anxious for more options and ready for the final step. In a gentle voice I say, "If we were releasing one of those lovely trout that we hooked this morning . . ." and as I tenderly get ahold of the fly right at the bend, I yank straight back. There is but one chance to do this, so it must be done with authority.

Part of the fun is viewing the abrupt emotional swings in the emancipated patient. Bug-eyed shock turns to relief in seconds. When the victim is hooked with a large fly or snagged in the delicates, you should think about using a piece of monofilament to remove the fly. The mono allows the hook to be pulled straight back.

Another Use for Duct Tape

Duct tape is marvelous for temporarily patching waders made of most materials, though not neoprene. It works so well I usually forget to patch the things properly and walk around with the tape on my high-dollar waders for half the season.

Chapter 4

CASTING

An endless number of books have been written on casting, so I'm not going to try to explain the mechanics. Others have done this better than I can. Casting is about feel, and I don't think casting instruction translates well into print anyway. (Video is a better medium.) But having watched and helped thousand of folks cast, I do have some observations that might be helpful.

Lessons

It is very important to take casting lessons, hopefully at the beginning of your fly-fishing career. Self-taught casters develop bad habits that can become deeply ingrained and hard to correct. I'm proof. I was a self-taught and ugly caster until I got help from two great instructors, Mel Krieger and Mike Atwell. I was so set in my inefficient ways that it took several years to retrain myself. I could not have changed my casting without an instructor holding my wrist and physically showing me a proper casting motion. Since then, I have realized that fly casting is so much about feel that people instinctively learn quicker if they keep their eyes *closed* during the demonstration. This way they can really concentrate on the little snap of the wrist that makes a good cast.

Something that really stands out in my mind after guiding thousands of fly fishers is that most people know only one type of cast—usually midrange. But several casts should be in every angler's repertoire.

The Tip Cast

A big trout rises a few feet away. You try to put the fly on the fish's head, but it lands on one side and, with the next cast, on the other side. Before you know it the prize has been spooked or wandered out of range without ever seeing the fly. Very few fly fishermen can throw the tight loop necessary to make short accurate casts. They bring the rod back too far or snap the wrist at the wrong time. The only way to get that sweet loop is by flexing the rod tip. The key to accomplishing that is learning the little snap of the wrist that flexes *just* the tip. Learning the tip cast is not easy, but it is the key to all good casts. All casts—long, short, and curved ones—are about bending the rod. A complete caster can utilize all the rod, from the butt right up to the tip. But the tip is the trickiest section to bend, and if you learn to flex it, the rest of your casting will fall into place.

Having an instructor physically show you is, of course, best, but if you can't get a lesson, here's a helpful exercise that will teach you this cast instinctively. Place a target 15 to 30 feet away, tie an inch of bright yarn on the end of your leader, and try to hit the target consistently. Your backcast should be very short and straight over your head. When I start folks on this drill, it

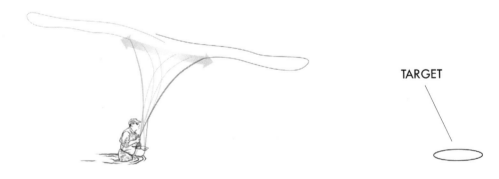

If you really want to learn how to cast, keep it short and on target

isn't long before they ignore the target and start shooting line "a-way-out-yonder." They seem so pleased with themselves that I hate to burst their bubble and tell them midrange casting is easy. If you *really* want to improve your casting, stay on target with the short cast. This exercise will cause you to tighten your loop and teach you that all-important flick of the wrist. It's the only way you will hit the target consistently.

The next time you're on the water try casting under trees or brush. This will teach you to instinctively throw a tight loop. This is certainly a more interesting classroom than the lawn, and if you should haul a fish out of such a great spot, the reward will cement the casting motion in your psyche. Over my years of guiding I have learned that nothing teaches better then success. When clients start catching fish, self-imposed barriers crumble, instincts takes over, and a fly fisherman is born.

The Midrange Cast

The midrange cast delivers flies medium distances and is used for a lot of trout fishing. During the casting stroke the rod flexes in the middle because it is brought from the old 10 to 2 o'clock positions. With the powerful rods of this day and age, the angle is really more like from 10:30 to 1:30. This cast is fine for throwing one or two unweighted flies, but when other items are attached to your leader, such as strike indicators and weight, the cast needs to be modified.

Slinging Lead

If you are slinging lead, a regular cast will get you lots of tangles. When all that junk is cast with a tight loop, the weight and air resistance make the terminal tackle collapse onto the line, creating a mess. Each stroke you make adds more complications to the bird's nest.

The solution to this misery is to make the cast in a wide arc. The goal is to keep everything tight with no slack spots in the

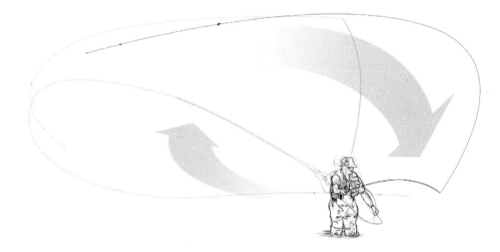

When slinging lead, start the cast with a powerful enough motion so that the "junk" will sail around on a tight line.

leader to cause trouble. The rod tip should actually go in an oval rather then the usual straight line. Start the cast with a strong enough snap so the line has sufficient power to complete the loop. Grab a piece of rope and sling it round and round cowboy-style over your head. Then envision what it would take to do this with a fly rod. It's a similar motion.

The Big Cast

In spending several years in the Bahamas chasing bonefish over the breezy flats, I learned that an oval motion sends the fly into the wind better than a traditional overhead cast. The oval, however, should not be as pronounced as the oval used for casting the nymph rig. When the cast is properly executed, the line will pass underneath your casting arm on the backcast and above the rod on the forecast, as a traditional cast would.

This is accomplished by bringing the arm back lower on the backcast than you normally would.

While guiding in the salt I discovered that most clients,

An oval casting motion slices into the wind better than a standard cast.

accustomed to casting for trout, couldn't generate enough power to get any distance. They had never learned to bend the rod right down to the handle. I would have the same problem at the beginning of each saltwater fly-fishing season, and it always took a couple of weeks before I developed a powerful stroke. All trout fishermen should do a lot of practicing well before any seaside adventure. Even better, have somebody show you how.

The Curved Cast
The curved cast is another important tool for the stream fly fisher. For example, a fisherman may be standing in the slow water on the inside of a bend, and the fish are in the current just off the bank. A straight cast will put most of the line and leader in the slower water, and only the fly will drop into the faster water. Consequently, you get a very short float because the part that is in the faster water quickly swings around and drags. You will get a better drift if everything is in the *same speed of current*.

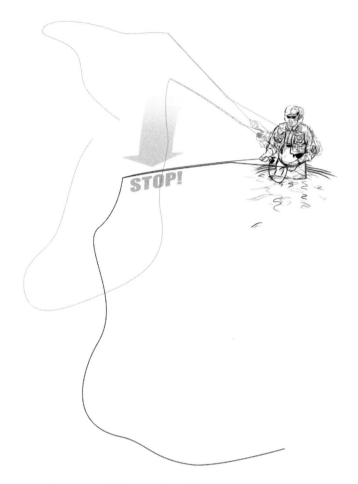

A curved cast can help you drop fly, line, and leader all in the same current—giving you a good float.

Although wading into a more favorable position is the best option, this isn't always possible, making a curved cast the next best solution. It is done by making a powerful sidearm cast and stopping the rod short. This shocks the rod and sends the end of the line, leader, and fly around in a curve. Many anglers have difficulty with this because they don't have a strong enough cast to overpower the forward stroke.

The Bad Cast

Unfortunately, the bad cast comes naturally for a lot of folks. It's actually a great tool to use when fishing upstream on fast-falling creeks where only short casts are required. The bad cast is easy enough; just perform one of several casting infractions: break your wrist, reach, or best of all, don't put any snap in the forward stroke. That will bring the rod down flat, which takes the bend out of the rod and puts slack in the line and leader, giving you a longer drag-free float than a proper straight cast would.

Backhandling

When fishing upstream it is best for a right-hander to be on the left side of the river. That way the cast falls to your right, and you can fish the drift out with the rod staying in that comfortable position. Stream geography, however, often places you on the other side of the river. This is a more awkward position because the line will drift down on the side of you opposite the rod, and you will have to fish across your body. If you use a conventional over-the-shoulder cast in this situation, you will make a cross-stream presentation. You can mend to improve the drift, but mending should always be a last resort, and it is usually better to backhand the cast.

Three Backhand Casts

Backhanding drops your cast at a more favorable angle, giving you more of a straight upstream presentation. It also puts the rod

When fishing up the "wrong side" of a stream, backhand the cast.

Few anglers are aware of how they backhand a cast. Most do it with the thumb up, as shown. Credit: Wes Edling.

in a better position to start the drift, and your line, leader, and fly will be in the same current. There are three different ways to backhand the cast, which can best be described by how the rod is held, referring to the position of the thumb.

(Keep in mind that the proper grip on the rod is with the thumb on top of the handle, opposite the guides.)

The first position for backhanding a cast is with the thumb up. This is the most common way anglers backhand a cast, but it is a weak stroke because the arm and shoulder can't get into the motion. Consequently the rod is merely waved in front, and the delivery will pile up. Try this motion, and the others to be described, with your hand now. You'll get a better idea of the points made here.

The second way to backhand a cast is by bringing the backcast over your left shoulder, understanding that all these directions are for right-handers, and the opposite is true for lefties. The thumb should come straight toward and almost touch the left

The number two backhand cast is good for casting dries at relatively close range. Credit: Wes Edling.

A sidearm cast, with the thumb horizontal, generates a lot of power. Credit: Wes Edling

shoulder. This cast is best for short-distance accuracy because the forward stroke is much the same as a conventional cast, where you are looking and aiming at your target. Incidentally, you can get more power out of the cast if you lean back on the backcast. That gives you a longer stroke, and consequently, a more powerful cast.

The third backhand cast gives you by far the most power, but you sacrifice accuracy. This cast is done with the thumb facing right, like a hitchhiker's. Technically, this is not a backhand cast but, instead, a conventional sidearm stroke, where the backcast is used as the forecast. I have had good luck teaching this by instructing anglers to turn around and *pretend* that they are casting downstream. I tell them to look back upstream when they drop the cast. This is a powerful motion because the whole arm and shoulder are behind the rod and driving it. Incidentally, this is also a handy cast for when the wind is blowing at a right angle into your casting arm. Just turn around and use the backcast as the forecast and it will put the line on the lee side of your body and prevent your getting hooked.

The Water Load

The water load is the ticket if you are fishing tight streams with brush on the banks. The advantage is that the fly spends very little time in the air, where the troublesome trees lurk. It is also a good cast to use when a sunken fly is drifted below you, because in such a situation you already have enough line out for the next drift and you needn't make a false cast. Let the current do the work. When the line straightens out below you, it loads the rod, and line, leader, tippet, and fly can be flung back upstream with an easy motion. The rod should be angled well back toward the

A smooth and easy motion sends the fly back upstream.

fly, but not quite at it. Then the submerged fly should be lifted slowly to the surface by raising the rod. When the weight of the line is felt pulling steadily against the rod, a smooth and easy stroke will send it upstream. If brush is a problem, the cast can be kept very low to the water. People often tend to put too much energy into this lob. To maximize its effectiveness, make sure that the fly is at the surface when you start the stroke.

Left-Right Finesse

When a right-hander is fishing upstream to his left, the fly drifts down on his left side, making it awkward to start a new cast from

Start with the rod to your left, swing it back around so that it ends up pointed over your right shoulder, then start your next cast. Do this maneuver slowly so the fly has a chance to drift past you.

that position. Why? Because the fly is on his left, the rod is on his right, and he will be bringing the fly across his body, putting himself in the precarious position of possibly hooking himself when he starts his cast. If you find yourself in this situation, you can get out of the predicament ever so gracefully by putting the rod over your head. Start with the rod to your left, swing it back around until it ends up pointed over your right shoulder, and then proceed with the next cast. Do this slowly so that the fly has a chance to drift away from you. Think of it as a cowboy throwing a rope, making a circle over his head.

Another Helpful Cast

Here is another slick move that can keep you and your guide from getting hooked and tangled with fly and line. If you are fishing upstream, as most anglers do, with too much slack, and try to start a new cast, the result can be reckless and sloppy. Rectify the situation by making a little forward flip or roll cast to get the line in the air and under control. When the roll cast straightens out in front of you, it loads the rod for the backcast.

If you find yourself with too much slack line, start your cast with a roll cast.

Critique Your Cast

You can judge your own casting if you watch—and listen. A rod that is properly cast makes very little sound; a rod that doesn't bend, however, makes a *whooshing* noise. The equally sinister

That's too far back!

sight of the fly and leader unrolling after the line is on the water will usually accompany this audio atrocity.

Too Far Back!

A common problem with casters is breaking the wrist and bringing the rod back too far. I have repeated the phrase, "Too far back!" to thousands of fly fishers in my life, with little more to show for it than a wrinkled brow and sore throat. My frustration has forced me to develop a new casting exercise that is extreme and controversial, but a foolproof way of correcting this most common of casting faults. All that is required is a very expensive fly rod and a fence that stands 3 or 4 feet higher than you. Simply stand 1 or 2 feet in front of the fence, with your back to it, and then proceed to cast. Your backcast should sail over the fence. Here I insert my disclaimer that neither I nor the publisher is responsible for broken fly rods. If your rod breaks against the fence, rest assured that you went "too far back."

The floating arm and shoulder is a common problem with the self-taught and can cause the whooshing sound. Instead of anchoring the rod, the caster pushes the rod back and forth on a horizontal plane and doesn't bend the rod. It accomplishes little but giving the caster's upper arm and shoulder a mighty workout. This caster's body rocks to and fro when he has to cast any distance, and if he's in the water his little dance will send alarming waves in all directions. A good casting stroke is more up and down than front and back. The rod should be *pulled* downward rather than *pushed* forward.

Many, if not most, fly fishers "reach" at the end of the cast. I have also noticed that the reacher is often guilty of too much false casting. He wings the line back and forth with greater intensity on each stroke. When the lay-down is anticipated, he sabotages it by reaching out with the arm. The subconscious is at work here, telling the caster that reaching will get him more distance. The opposite is true: Power is lost when the arm is extended at the end of the cast.

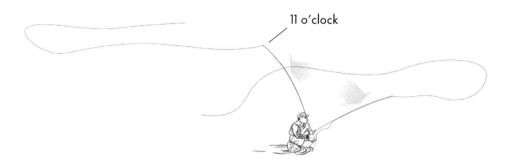

11 o'clock

When casting in a wind, shift your casting stroke from 10—2 o'clock to 11—3 o'clock. This will break the cast right over the water and the wind can't play with the fly.

It is very simple to tell if you are a reacher; just see where your arm is positioned when the cast is completed. If your elbow is down and the rod is straight out in front you at the conclusion of the cast, you've done it right. If your arm winds up extended, you've done it wrong. I'm forever correcting casters while they are fishing. Helping them to get rid of the reach is not too hard, but it tends to creep back with each stroke, and after a few minutes their arm ends up extended again.

Another common casting fault is that most casters have far too little range of motion and cramp their cast into a short stroke where their hand only travels a foot or so. If your casts don't turn over all the way, or they come down hard, this may be the cause. If you can learn to let the arm ride upward, it will open up your stroke and improve your casting immensely.

False Cast with Patience

Modern times in America have produced a new sort of fly-casting problem. Some folks are in such a hurry to have fun that they don't wait for the line to straighten out when false casting. It takes longer than you think for that line to straighten out behind you, so wait.

Chapter 5

WATER AND WEATHER CONDITIONS

Getting on the water when conditions are right is probably the most important ingredient in successful trout fishing. All the gear, ability, and knowledge in the world won't amount to a hill of beans if the fish are inactive. We'll never know *exactly* what gets them going, but the clever angler pays attention to the air and water, and learns, over time, which combination of conditions produces the best fishing.

When you have to make a living outguessing Mother Nature's finicky ways, you pay really close attention. Here are some conclusions I have come to after decades of stalking the wily trout and the even more elusive greenback.

Travel with Knowledge

Anglers who live close to their fishing should have a different plan than those who have to travel to get to the water. Folks who fish in their own neighborhood have a big advantage, because they don't have to waste time pounding the stream when conditions are bad.

If you have to travel to fish, knowing what shape the river is in before you get there is of great benefit. Water conditions are forever changing: it's too high and muddy, too low and clear, it's too hot, too cold—always something. So be sure to do some homework before setting out. Call fly shops and use the Internet to get the latest information. Most important, be flexible. Don't embrace rigid notions: "I'm going to fish the Big Muddy in June." The Big Muddy might be too clear in June. Always have a "Plan B" waiting in the wings.

Canyon streams generally fish better when the water is low.

Flow Rate

Flow rates for rivers throughout the United States can be accessed at www.water.usgs.gov/realtime.html. This Web site provides you with measurements from those little tin silos you see along our rivers, and it enables you not only to find out the up-to-the-minute flow rate for a river but also to see the trend, that is, whether the water is rising or falling. Of course, this type of information is of value only if you know what you're looking for. A rate of 100 cubic feet per second will be meaningless unless you know at what level the river fishes best. Call the nearest fly shop and ask what conditions they prefer. If you do go and find the water to your liking, check the flow rate on the Web site when you get home so you have a reference point for the future.

Temperature and Time of Day

If the water is warm, trout, especially the bruisers, don't feed well. If the water is too cold, the fish act like a kid with a plate full of vegetables: They pick and nibble. You can have good fishing when the water is running hot or cold, however, by choosing the right time of day. I often have been on my way to fish around midmorning and run into a discouraged, tired fisherman on his way back in. He had hit the water with a vengeance at dawn. It sounds so promising to be out there before breakfast, but from my experience, the best trout fishing occurs at midday. Insects usually become active in midmorning, and the trout's appetite seems to peak at about 1 P.M. The extremely knowledgeable Roderick Haig-Brown came to the same conclusion, but added another explanation for midday success. In his wonderful book, *A River Never Sleeps*, Haig-Brown wrote, "You know that a fisherman will probably do his best work then too." I don't know about you, but I'm a little slow on the trigger at sunup.

When the air is very cool, the fish will feed late in the day, after the water has had a chance to warm. This makes for some predictable, and consequently good, fishing. The volume of a stream is a factor. Larger streams will be less affected by air temperature swings than smaller streams.

Conversely, if the weather is warmer than normal, the fish will start feeding earlier in the day. (In the heat of midsummer, that might be daybreak.)

Direction of Flow

The direction of flow is another consideration when planning to fish a particular river. For instance, small streams with spooky trout fish best if you have the sun at your back. Consequently, those that flow west will usually fish best in the last half of the day.

High Water

Trout don't want to battle big currents, so look for them where they can escape heavy flows, which is usually at the edges. When choosing an area to fish where water levels are high, look for sections of river with a lot of bends; the inside of these bends will have

When dealing with rising or high water, winding sections will usually provide more holding water than straight stretches of river.

slack water and high concentrations of fish. If you are not familiar with a river, study maps and head for the windiest sections.

Low Water

High water tends to spread fish out toward the edges, but low water concentrates trout in holes. If air and water temperatures are high, the fish will be thick below oxygenated white water. Last season on the Rio Grande in New Mexico, the water was miserably low and warm. A waterfall pool that had a half mile of flat water on either side of it attracted every fish in the neighborhood. They were packed in like sardines. Because the Rio is a large river, the trout didn't spook from the commotion of a fish fighting, making it easy to catch one right after another.

Rising Water

It is rare to be on the river when the water is rising rapidly due to precipitation, but trout can go on quite a rampage then, because the first stages of a rise will carry lots of debris, including food, before the water actually turns dirty. Areas that are freshly inundated with water may draw trout that are on the hunt for food.

In tailwaters, a rise in the flow will usually turn off fish. If the tailwaters have been low and the fish have been crowded in the holes, however, a rise often triggers mass appetites. But be patient as they usually shuffle around stretching their fins for a half hour or so before they start eating.

Discolored Water

Fly fishermen hate dirty and muddy water, and I'm no exception. This says more about our attitude, however, than about the feeding habits of fish. After all, no matter the color of the water, they have to eat. Actually, water with some color to it often fishes better than clear water, because trout feel safe when it is a little murky and will venture into the shallows to feed. If there is over a foot of visibility, they can find grub—and your fly—just fine. When the visibility is reduced down to inches, however, their feeding strategy changes, because they are unable to see insects drifting by their lie. They will feed more on the bottom, and since they can't find much to eat, they will lose weight. Dead drifting and jigging big, heavy, high-visibility flies, such as black or orange Krystal Flash Woolly Buggers, seem to be the best tactics in muddy water.

Clearing and Dropping Water

Clearing and dropping water puts trout on the feed. Often the best fishing of the season is when the spring runoff is winding down. Water temperatures are usually perfect then, and insect hatches are at their peak. In addition, the fish haven't been harassed since the previous year.

If the water level has been on the high side, tailwater fish almost always respond favorably when the river is lowered. Check flow rates on the Internet and grab the gear when the level plummets.

Normal Flows

I mention normal flows last for a reason. With logging, irrigation, grazing, years of poor fire management, and summer homes everywhere, very few watersheds function the way God intended. All that abuse causes rivers to rise and fall drastically. Consequently, most waterways in the United States run at optimum, bank-to-bank levels only between flood and drought. On these joyous occasions, trout will be smiling and will spread out in the river.

High or Low?

Some rivers fish well when the water is low, others when the water is high. Generally, deeper canyon streams and large rivers fish better under low-water conditions, because the fish become easier to get at. Smaller, shallower watercourses usually fish best when running brim full. This is unquestionably true in the area of Argentina where I fish, from Bariloche north to the town of Alumine. The huge Lemay, Collon Cura, and Alumine rivers fish poorly when they are swollen, and the smaller rivers, like the Traful and Malleo, need plenty of fluid because the trout live under the willows and become homeless if the water shrinks back from the bank. Just like anywhere, if they have someplace better to go, they go. That is why sections of rivers in Argentina near lakes may produce poor fishing in summer; the trout move to the lakes when river conditions deteriorate.

Altitude

In the areas with which I am most familiar—the steep mountains of New Mexico, Colorado, and Argentina—the altitude varies greatly, and streams blossom at different times. The cold-running waters at high elevations fish best in summer, and the waters at lower elevations fish best in the cool seasons: spring, fall, and even winter.

You can apply this same principle to determine where to fish during short-term weather changes. If a cold front hits, head downriver, where the water will be warmer. If the weather turns hot, go upstream. A good rule of thumb is to go where the temperature is the most comfortable for you; the fish will most likely agree with your choice.

Weather and Light

Weather is a big factor in any type of fishing. Exactly what fishing corresponds to what weather is hard to pin down, but sometimes it just smells fishy. This is not as far out a statement as you might think, because our noses work well when the air is still, humid, and overcast. Those also happen to be the best conditions for most insect hatches.

Blue Skies

Bright blue skies are what we fish under a lot in the southern Rockies, and although plenty of trout are caught in sunlight, fish and insects usually prefer shade. I experienced this recently on the Rio Grande. The Rio winds through a deep canyon with vertical cliffs, and on this clear day, in the midst of a great caddis hatch, no fish were rising. We were catching trout on nymphs, but, of course, we wanted to use dries, and I knew a place where an overhanging cliff would be casting a shadow on the river. When we got there, the few square yards of shaded water were crowded with risers.

Dusky Light

The dusky light trout love doesn't have to come from the setting of the sun. The same light can be found when clouds move in or when the sun hangs low in the sky during spring and fall. I once spent a couple of days fishing under the smoke of a forest fire. It was odd: the air was orange, big white ash fell all around, and the insects and fish rose into the never-ending twilight all day long.

Cold Front

The dreaded cold front almost always puts fish off—any fish, anyplace. Just before a front hits in hot weather, especially in the fall, however, the opposite occurs, often producing excellent fishing. Some nastiness associated with these systems, such as falling snow, can put trout on the feed. Once the front pushes through the area, the fish usually sulk until the weather warms. If the water gets too cold, follow the weather carefully and fish a day or two after the temperature rebounds.

Thunderstorms

For several years, I guided on a ranch that featured a lodge overlooking a creek and a series of ponds. When not on the water, we would sit on the deck of the lodge and scan the nearest pond for feeding trout. It was shallow, and the fish were surface oriented, so if no fish were rising, they weren't eating. In midsummer, it was common for thunderstorms to build midday, vent wind, rain, and lightning and then move on. Over the course of several seasons, the trout's feeding habits as those storms blew through became clear from our observatory. Since then, I have noticed the same tendencies during violent weather elsewhere.

When a thunderstorm was building, the fish were active, especially if there was cloud cover. When the wind started blowing, the feeding eased off. When the air really swirled, the fish would sulk. The lull usually lasted through the storm, but the trout would go back to feeding if the wind abated. The cloudy, humid calm after the storm was a very good time to fish.

Rain

Trout love rain, and although fishing can be good in a downpour, it is almost always excellent in a light and steady drizzle—as long as there is little or no wind. The wind throws that unsettled component back into the equation and usually turns off the fish.

Sun, Shade, and Silhouette

Experienced hunters instinctively use sun and shadow to their advantage. They naturally gravitate toward places where they have a lighting advantage over their prey. We fly fishermen don't need to function on that level of awareness, but we would catch and release more fish if we used light and shade to our advantage.

First and foremost, try to position the sun behind you in all fishing situations. You will have a better view of the fish, your fly, and the bottom. Of even greater importance is that the wary trout is less likely to see you when the sun is behind you. Contrarily, when you are looking into the sun, the fish can see you, but you can't see it.

Keeping this in mind when approaching nervous fish, angle around until you can head in from a favorable direction. Don't blind yourself by looking up to figure out where the yellow ball is; just glance at your shadow and aim it toward the fish. Yes, your shadow cast over the fish would spook it, but this is only a concern when the sun is so low in the sky that your shadow is very long.

Fishing with the sun in your favor is such a big factor in certain waters, such as small streams with slow pools, I sometimes

When approaching a fish, try to position yourself so that the sun is at your back. As you move, gradually get lower and lower until you are in a full crouch.

Stay close to cover, even when watching for feeding fish.

won't even bother fishing places where I am forced to fish with the sun in my eyes. Keep score of how you do with a low-slanting sun behind you and how you do with the sun in front of you. The results will prove the importance of keeping the light behind you whenever possible.

If you have the sun in your favor, you may be able to approach delicate water standing upright. If, however, the fish have a good chance of seeing you, get down. Trout can spook from a very long way off when you are highlighted against the sky, so look behind you and see if you are silhouetted. If you are, get down or utilize surrounding cover. Although anglers accustomed to fishing small streams are all too familiar with groveling on their knees to catch fish, many arrive upright and then get down. Start your approach with a walking crouch; gradually stoop lower and lower as you approach the water. That way your profile stays at the same height as you move into your final position.

On smaller streams, it is hard to catch more than one fish out of a tranquil pool under low-water conditions. If, however, you stay low and don't stand up to land fish, the others might not spook and may be fooled as well.

Fishermen in the shade are much less likely to be spotted than those in the sun. The ideal setup is for the fish to be in the sunlight while you are lurking in the shadows. When the fish is in the shade and you are in the sun, it's "Advantage—Fish."

So, whenever possible, position yourself in the shadow of a tree, bush, or boulder. It is generally wise to stay close to such cover, because standing in front of or next to a bush, regardless of the shadow factor, breaks up your silhouette.

If my clients are having poor luck fishing small mountain streams under favorable conditions, I always assume the trout are getting spooked and resort to more stealth. A combination of planning the approach more carefully, keeping a low profile, and staying farther back does the trick.

Chapter 6

FISHING PRESSURE

Any modern book about trout fishing in America has to cover fishing pressure and how to deal with the stressed breed of fish—and fisherman—that it produces. Catch and release has made for some wonderful fishing, but many people make the erroneous assumption that released trout are easily captured again. Fish that have recently been molested become difficult to fool; they just don't like being caught.

Early-season trout, and those that are seldom fished for, will rise with abandon to gulp just about any fly, and unless they are in the midst of an intense hatch, such innocent trout are not naturally very selective. Once we have harassed them, however, they become problematic and may even develop quirks. These quirks can vary from place to place; I know of one creek where the fish, in reaction to fishing pressure, have learned to spit flies out incredibly fast. Sometimes they become extremely spooky and highly selective. Heavy angling pressure can change their dining habits too; trout learn that it is safer to eat subsurface and under low-light conditions.

New Mexico's San Juan River harbors examples of highly selective fish. There, the tremendous number of big rainbows is nearly equaled by the number of fishermen pursuing them. Trout so besieged develop nervous habits, and the key to catching them is getting in tune with their quirks. Their little lunacies can be very subtle, and you may be standing next to someone who is catching one right after the other, while you fish the same water in apparently the same manner with apparently the same fly and

A guide can make a big difference when you're fishing for highly selective, pressured fish. Credit: Peter Lloyd

catch nothing. One day the trout are eating only No. 26 olive midge pupae presented just so, while the following day—or hour—they prefer a presentation and fly just a hair different. This gives you one big uphill climb if you are new on the block. Of course, in this type of situation a guide can make all the difference in the world, and if you can afford to hire one, it will pay off.

Woolly Bugger Them

If you are without a guide, you may be able to even the playing field by "Woolly Buggering" them, as my son Nick calls it. When he is faced with temperamental, pain-in-the-ass fish, he doesn't stand there for hours scratching his head and picking through his fly box. Instead of being suckered in by an individual fish that may be nearly impossible to apprehend, Nick pounds the river with Woolly Buggers. By covering a lot of fish, he finds plenty of takers.

Actually, there are many times when you may do better

Woolly Buggering them than by matching the hatch. I remember one still and misty morning on a lake in southern Colorado when a huge midge hatch came off. The fish were rising everywhere, but I was having little luck getting any of them to see and take my minuscule imitation amongst the gazillion flies. I switched to a black Woolly Bugger, dragged it in front of those rising fish, and caught one after another.

The Right Fly Can Be Paramount
Many times, of course, having the right fly is paramount, but plenty has been written on that subject, so I'm not going to wade into that crowded pool. Here's a different angle: After years of fishing and guiding, I bother less and less with trying to match the hatch—especially if the fish are big and the flies are small, because it is difficult to land heavy fish on tiny hooks and thin leaders. So, when fish are feeding on No. 22 trico nymphs, I usually have my client use a No. 16 short-shanked Bead-Head Hare's Ear Nymph (or Copper John, Pheasant Tail, et al) on 4X tippet because that size hook and tippet will land large fish handily. In most streams, the fish eat so many flies of that size and color that they just grab the little morsel as it goes by out of habit. Furthermore, the larger fly will be seen more easily by the fish than the tiny, numerous trico nymphs.

My son Nick recently told me an interesting anecdote. He was fishing the Clarks Fork in Montana and was having a hard time with the fish, even though he had been given the "right fly" by a friend of his who guides on the river. The fish, however, didn't seem to know that he was fishing the right fly and refused it. So, he changed flies—again and again until he wound up with the same fly with which he began, when he finally started catching fish. He deduced that he would have been better off to have kept putting the one recommended fly over the fish than fussing with all those flies.

When he told me this little story I started to think of the

hundreds of times I've done the same thing. Selective trout can be like that; you just have to put your fly over them repeatedly, and maybe on the fiftieth pass they'll eat it. Incidentally, "over them" does not mean a foot or two away; practice your tip casting until you can aim that fly into the fish's mouth.

Other Anglers Are a Problem

Dealing with other anglers is a big factor on our crowded streams these days. Part of the problem may lie with differences in perspective. Folks from urban areas are used to being elbow to elbow and may actually volunteer their company for other anglers' benefit. Tension arises when these fishermen encounter crusty hicks like me who secretly hate all "foreigners" encountered on "my water."

This animosity has validity on small creeks where the angler's greatest concern is spooking fish. If someone is fishing in front of you, you aren't going to catch anything. You should never fish behind another angler on small streams with wild trout if you can avoid it. To tell if there is someone fishing ahead of you, be on the lookout for water splashed up on rocks. Tumbling water splashes water on rocks, of course, but the clumsy feet of "foreigners" splash it higher. It probably takes 20 minutes to a half-hour for those splashes to evaporate, which is about the same amount of time it takes spooked fish to return to feeding.

If you see such signs, don't continue fishing, for the fish are likely to be spooked anyway. Instead, find the other angler and watch him for a couple of minutes to find out who it is and what he's up to. If, for instance, it's a beginner moving fast, you may want to relax a few minutes and let him fish on ahead. The neophyte only frightens the trout, and they will get back to normal once the crashing and splashing have stopped. You wouldn't, however, want to follow a really skilled angler. He will scour all the best water and hook many fish. Conversely, if the competition is moving slowly, you may want to go around and move up ahead. You certainly don't want to get into a jogging match from pool to pool; go far enough above him so that he doesn't have to fish your tainted water.

It is also usually a good policy to talk to the other angler because he may have thought he had the river all to himself and may feel resentment at your intrusion. Having a little chat may break the tension. Maybe you can find out some pertinent information, such as where the other angler has been fishing, how he has fared, and so on. Ask if there are others in his party and where they are. Ask about his plans and then try to work out a simple arrangement that keeps everybody in good water.

No matter what your approach is to meeting others on the water, common sense and courtesy dictate that you leave everyone else plenty of elbow room. The amount of room will vary widely according to the degree of congestion. On some waters, that may be just a couple of casts away, whereas in really remote places the appropriate distance between anglers could be a mile or more. Dealing with other fishermen is part of trout fishing, and the more tactful your conduct, the brighter the day.

Chapter 7

HATCHES

It's great to be on the water during a good hatch, but I don't make that big a deal out of targeting specific hatches. Maybe that has to do with the nature of guiding. We don't say to the client, "The pale morning dun hatch starts at 11 A.M. and lasts for about an hour, so we can wrap it up by noon." No, we fish all day, through the good, the bad, and the ugly. What I'm really interested in is the general activity on the water throughout the day. If there is life abuzz and bugs in the air, the trout are far more likely to be feeding, whether or not they are eating a particular insect.

During multiple hatches some fish may feed on one insect while others are partial to a different one. This is because certain insects are more available in particular portions of a stream, and the fish that live in those places eat what's put on the table. For instance, caddisflies swarm near brush and crawl around streamside, so trout look for them there. Most mayflies, however, hatch in shallow riffles and then free-float downriver. The fish will be looking for those morsels below riffles and in areas where surface debris is funneled. Midges are thickest over silty bottoms.

The intensity of the hatch is also a factor, because although you might see many small mayflies float by before the trout become interested in them, the sighting of one stonefly is enough evidence to tie on an imitation one—because often the largest trout in the river key on that big insect.

On rare occasions there are too many natural insects, and the trout have too many choices. This is when you need to repeatedly put your fly right over the fish. It is a good idea to use two

When hatches are very prolific—like this caddis hatch—try to catch the hatch early, before fish become jaded.

flies here; one an exact imitation of the insect, and the other one being just a little different than the natural. Sometime they will prefer the odd one for some reason.

Timing Counts

The timing of hatches should be considered too. Too bad all aquatic insects aren't as predictable and dependable as the pale morning dun. On a day-to-day basis, however, hatches *are* predictable on a given river, as long as conditions stay the same. If conditions change, adjustments can be made. For example, if the blue winged olive hatch normally starts at 3 P.M., and a cold front moves into the area, the hatch will most likely come off late. These daily predictable hatches create the scenario that gives up really good fishing. In reality, many hatches are just encountered by chance, and by the time you find the right fly, the party is already over. If you know when the flies are coming off, you can not only have the right imitation on, but be at the right place at the right time.

Chapter 8

"STRIKE!"

I was recently in the fly shop down the street—Los Rios Anglers in Taos, New Mexico—talking to owner John Rainey about guiding. John had a client the day before who knew his entomology and had all the right gear, but couldn't hook any fish. John, being the astute guide that he is, stood back a few paces and tried to see if he could figure out the problem.

Set the Hook

From a distance John could see that when the man set the hook, his arm sprang straight up, but his rod stayed horizontal to the water. It was the dreaded "strike that ain't." This is a rather common problem and is perhaps a nervous reaction to experiencing the moment of truth. I've seen excitable clients jump straight up in the air at the sight of the fish taking the fly, and the "strike that ain't" is reminiscent of that.

Too much attention is paid to obscure and overrated aspects of fly fishing: leader formulas, persnickety fly design, subspecies of insects…the list is endless. Little, if anything, however, is ever mentioned about that instant action of utmost importance: setting the hook. After seeing thousands of fish missed because of late and faulty striking I can assure you that this overlooked aspect of fly fishing gets absolute top billing with me.

If you are going to hang on to a fish, the hook must be set. On hard-mouthed fish like tarpon this is a huge aspect. By contrast, we tend to think that the setting of a hook in a wee trout isn't important, but if you tend to lose fish after they have been

The dreaded "strike that isn't." The arm goes up, but the rod stays horizontal—the line never draws tight.

on for just a short time, it is likely that the hook point wasn't driven home in the first place. Hold a hook against your skin and imagine how much pressure it would take to bury it. It would be quite a bit. If you think you might not have sunk the fly in the fish's mouth when you initially struck, set the hook again while fighting the fish. Incidentally, a hook penetrates easier if the barb has been removed.

Use Enough Tippet

Of course, use a tippet heavy enough to match the job. You can't set a No. 6 Woolly Bugger with 6X tippet, although a lot of people try. I often guide beginners who invariably have several spools of terribly thin tippet. The neophyte, as well as the clerk who sold him the stuff, believes that trout are such clever creatures that anglers had better play it safe and use only 6X. The truth is that such frail line is seldom prudent and people can usually use much heavier tippets than they do. An exception would be certain tailwaters and spring creeks, where the flies are tiny and the fishing pressure is great. I use 3X and 4X for most of my fishing. I believe 5X is for flies under No. 18, and 2X is usually okay for streamers.

Detecting the Bite

You have more time to set the hook on a big fish than on a small one. It simply takes longer for a fly to travel in and out of a bucketmouth. When the hook is set into a large fish it is being driven into something solid that doesn't give. So your terminal tackle sets—and breaks—easily. Small trout, on the other hand, may simply be pulled toward you when the hook set is attempted and they are never actually hooked.

If every nymph fisherman knew how many undetected and missed strikes he had in the course of a day, it would change the way he fished forever. Whenever possible, I take up a position well above the stream so that I can spot fish for my client. When the client is casting a nymph to an individual fish, I have found it is better for me to watch the fish rather than the indicator. When I assume the fly is in the neighborhood of the trout I look for it to move or open its mouth. I then screech, "Strike! at the top of my lungs.

This is by no means foolproof, because the fish may not be eating the nymph. Instead, it might just be scratching itself, but results over the years have proven it is better for me to watch the fish rather than the indicator, because very often the indicator never moves when the trout eats the fly.

Most fly fishermen have the notion that trout take food in various fashions. The moody rascals "nail it" sometimes and "take real gently" at other times. It's true that when they are very hungry or chasing moving prey, they take assertively—and on those occasions they are easier to hook. Conversely, when they are not so hungry, they tend to pick and nibble and are more difficult to latch onto. Since most of the food trout eat is free-floating and can't escape, however, fish usually inhale their meals rather leisurely, often drifting along with the fly as they eat it. Such a take *causes no hesitation in the path of the strike indicator.* Nor will the indicator react when a fish comes toward you to take the fly.

Think of the lazy trout eating like you do. He casually picks up a bug like you would a hamburger—it's not going anywhere. If the meal is about to get away, however, and is passing behind the trout in fast water, the fish may rush to get it before it washes away. (If your Big Mac slips out of your hands, you'll make a stab for it before it hits the floor.) Such a fish will be easy to hook because the indicator will race upstream as the animal heads back to its feeding station. The fly will probably not be ejected until the fish gets back there. Remember, however, that more often than not, a trout nonchalantly takes a fly that is passing next to it. Its little, uncluttered brain will notice that there is a hunk of metal hanging off the proposed meal, and he will eject the phony immediately, giving you only a fraction of a second to react.

To illustrate this point: I once had a client who wanted to go beyond catch and release—to strike and release—so we cut the hook off right at the bend. We were fishing for cutthroats in a stream that is heavily fished and those trout, after the first week of two of the season, spit the fly out incredibly fast. Those same trout grabbed the hookless fly and swam around the creek with it like a dog with a bone.

Recognize and React

Undoubtedly the two most costly mistakes nymph fishermen make are not recognizing a take and then not striking fast enough. This is especially true for beginning anglers who have not developed a level of concentration that is equal to the task. It is also true even for experienced fly fishers when they are not on their game. I know that when I'm tired I miss a lot of strikes. The indicator makes a slight jiggle; the event tours the foggy

This striking motion is poor because it pulls the fly out of the fish's mouth.

mind, and a decision is finally made to set the hook. *Too late!* The secret is to concentrate, and then when anything "funny" happens shoot first and ask questions later. Set that hook now! It is better to strike too fast and hard and break fish off now and then than to be too slow and miss them all.

When you are upstream nymph fishing in deep water, the most likely place you'll get a strike may be right beside or below you. This is where the fly is running the deepest and is the most effective. In this situation your rod should be moving at the same pace as your fly and downstream of it. The drift should be extended as far as possible by reaching below you. Unfortunately most anglers blow it when they get a strike from that position because they set the hook with the standard upward lift of the rod. That motion pulls the fly in the wrong direction—out of the fish's mouth. Furthermore, this upward motion slows contact because it changes the angle of the rod, forming slack between the rod tip and the fly. If the strike is made *downstream*, however, with a

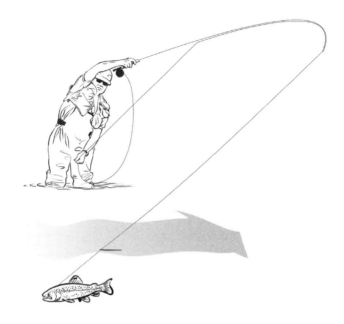

This is an efficient striking motion. The hook makes faster contact with the fish, and the angle promotes better hook penetration.

motion that is a continuation of the rod's downstream movement, you'll get the quickest contact between rod tip and fly.

When trout take a dry fly they rise up to eat it and don't eject it until they return to their feeding station. The best time to set the hook is when the fish is heading downward. Consequently a somewhat leisurely strike is best. If the dry is small—under No. 18—set the hook gently, especially if you are using a stiff rod, so the tiny gap doesn't rip through the fish's flesh.

Sight-Fishing Challenge

Sight fishing for big trout with dries is high drama. Because these bruisers rise in an unhurried manner, they give you plenty of time to get overamped, and it is really easy to set the hook too soon and too hard, when the fish's mouth is still open and facing upward. Wait for the jaws to close and then set the hook.

As Dave Ames notes in his book, *A Good Life Wasted,* slack is evil. There is no way this angler can pull everything tight and hook this fish.

Don't "Slack" Off

Most anglers are lazy about controlling their slack line and would hook a lot more fish if they were more prudent about taking it up. They often cease recovering line toward the end of the drift and wind up with the rod pointing skyward and slack at their feet. This makes it physically impossible for them to set the hook if a fish should take their fly in close quarters.

Dry Fly–Nymph Combo

The dry fly with a bead-head dropper below it is murder on trout, and if you can set the nymph quickly and the dry slowly, you will catch even more on this setup.

The "Let-Em-Take-It" Strike

I used to miss a lot of trout when retrieving a fly. Then I trolled a lake alone in a rowboat and learned the "let-em-take-it" strike. I discovered that when I was rowing and the rod was propped up in the stern and out of my hands I caught more fish than when I was holding the rod. When I had the rod in my hands I would set the hook at every little bump, but when manning the oars I couldn't respond to those "nibbles," and that allowed the fish to take the fly. Since then I have watched many trout follow retrieved flies. They often nip and tuck at them, especially Woolly Buggers, before they take. If you set the hook during one of those pecks, you are simply pulling the fly out of his sight. If you do miss a fish like that, cast back to it immediately. When swinging, retrieving, or trolling a fly, I try to resist the natural urge to strike when I feel something and wait until I feel the weight of the fish before setting the hook.

Complete the Retrieve

Finishing a retrieve so that you can make a curved-line strike really boosts hookup percentages. When the fly is fairly close, perhaps 20 feet away from you, raise the rod to complete the retrieve. Do this slowly and evenly so that the line gets a belly in it, and watch for that belly to tighten as the fly approaches you. If you see the line start to tighten, set the hook. When a fish grabs the fly on a slack line like that, hookup percentages soar. Unfortunately, fish can take flies very deep this way and may become gill hooked.

This is a good hooking technique when you are fishing sinking lines in lakes, because trout often follow the fly. If you lift the rod slowly, they have a chance to take it. Experience has taught me to not just rip a fly out of the water when it is well below the surface but swim it all the way to the top so that a following fish has a chance to get it.

Steady Beats Fancy

Steady retrieves hook more fish than fancy ones do. We all love to make twitches and pauses with the rod; they make us feel like we are cleverly enticing the trout, but over the long haul my clients catch more fish with long, steady pulls. When they make fancy retrieves, their hands or rods are engaged in some sort of gyration and consequently out of position to set the hook when a fish strikes. With long, steady pulls, however, my clients are always ready to react.

Short and Tight

Some fly fishermen inadvertently let line slide under their finger when they set the hook. If you are missing a lot of strikes—or fish come off after a short time—make sure you have the line clamped down under your finger when you set the hook.

Get Close

Whenever you have a choice, especially when nymph fishing, fish a short line. It's hard to hook fish consistently when there is a lot of line on the water. Perhaps all the stretch in a long length of fly line is part of the problem. Trout can spit flies out so quickly that I wonder if the speed of light doesn't come into play here, because like those stars that blow up "way out there," by the time we see it, it's already happened.

Chapter 9

CATCH MY DRIFT

The concept of dead drifting a dry fly or nymph is really very simple: The fly has to sail along in the current like a natural insect does—free-floating. This sounds easy, but doing it when the fly is attached to a leader is not. It would be a snap if all rivers flowed at an even pace from bank to bank, but if that were the case, trout fishing would be a dull game. Outwitting weaving currents keeps it interesting.

Using long, thin tippets helps a fly act natural, but long leaders are unwieldy, inaccurate to cast, and easy to break. They certainly aren't a cure-all for fooling trout. What usually gets you the best drift is having the line, leader, and fly all in the same current. Casting cross-stream subjects your line and leader to different currents, so fishing as straight upstream as possible is normally the best means to get a good drift. You can do several things to get the best float when fishing upstream: proper positioning, reaching, reach casting, high sticking, refloating, and mending.

Proper Positioning

Getting into proper position is the most desirable option, for it presents the simplest and most straightforward solution. Aggressive wading becomes important here, because getting into the ideal position can be difficult. I'm forever begging my clients to "wade out just a step further." The position you seek would allow you to place your fly straight upstream and just a little to your right if you are right-handed, to the left if you are

Point your rod tip at the fly and let it drift.

a southpaw. From that position, your fly, strike indicator, leader, and line are all in the same speed of current. As they drift downstream toward your rod tip, which is to your right, the rod should be pointed at the fly. When the fly gets within 25 feet, raise the rod to take up the remaining slack. That way you don't

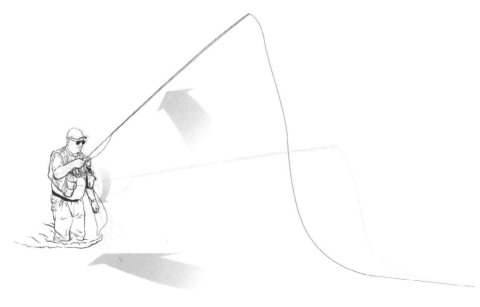

Toward the end of the drift slowly pick up slack by raising the rod.

have to take up all the slack by hand, and when the rod becomes vertical you will be in position to make the next cast, with enough line out of the rod so that it loads easily. Just as they do when "high sticking," anglers tend to lift the rod too soon, that is, when they have too much line on the water.

Raising the rod too soon not only causes the fly to drag but can also create excess slack between rod tip and fly. If there is slack *and* the rod is in a vertical position, it is impossible to tighten the line and set the hook.

Reaching

Unfortunately, ideal positioning is seldom easy to obtain. Rivers are often too deep, fast, and wide for you to get where you need to be, in which case the next best option is getting as close as you can to that position and "reach." Reaching is the solution when there is a different speed current between you and your fly, but you have to be close enough to that current so that you can lift the line out of the flow. The longer the rod here the better. By raising the rod, you can lift the line off the water, reposition it elsewhere, and even add a mend at the same time.

Reach Cast

A reach can be applied when a cast is being laid down and is sensibly called the reach cast. It is a little tricky to perform because the reach needs to be applied as the line is falling to the water. Consequently, the cast needs to be deadened to allow time for the rod to be maneuvered right or left during the line's descent.

High Sticking

Even though the term high sticking sounds more appropriate in a sports bar, it is an accurate description of a fly-fishing maneu-ver. It is really just reaching out with the extended arm to lift the

You'll catch more fish by keeping your fly in the water. When drifting through a prime stretch, raise and lower the rod instead of making time-consuming casts.

line and leader off the water and follow it downstream. Remember that this maneuver is for *short lines only*. Anglers get too fond of this high sticking business and often try it when their fly is too far away. Furthermore, few make full use of their arm the way they could. The appendage can be extended to make that 9-foot rod a longer and better tool, but instead, the arm usually hangs limp at the angler's side. As much as I hate to cast aspersions, my observations lead me to conclude that the average fly fisher is a lazy cuss.

Refloating

When you are wade fishing you can daydream, rest, or look at the birds. When you wake up, you'll be in the same spot. In the fast game of float-fishing quick rivers, however, each false cast you make takes your fly out of the water and past another likely spot. You can get your fly more playing time without casting by refloating it. When the fly's drift has been exhausted it will be below the boat and starting to drag. Refloat the fly by lifting the rod to vertical—or past vertical—then maneuver the line this

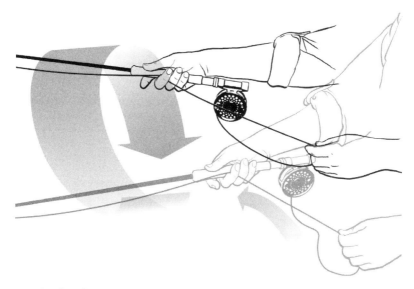

Mend only when necessary.

way or that, upstream of where you think a fish is. The rod is then lowered, and the fly can be fished again for a few feet.

Mending

Many situations may call for "mending." Used indiscriminately, the technique can be detrimental. If a fish decides to take just as a mend is being performed, the angler will invariably miss the strike because the hands and mind are busy. People get in the *habit* of mending because they fish a particular river where it is necessary to mend. On some waters, guides have their clients throw mends on each cast. Because it's a good idea for some rivers, however, doesn't mean it's a good idea elsewhere. The worst offense is the obligatory mend that is thrown just after the fly lands. (Eastern fly fishers are very prone to this.) This is often the exact time a fish jumps on a fly, and by tossing a superfluous mend, the angler may either pull the fly out of the action or put himself out of position to set the hook. I hesitate to show clients how to mend because they

Whenever possible, have your rod tip over the water you are fishing so that the current can't grab the line.

often become enamored with throwing those cute little loops and then start flipping the line all over the place! Use the operation only when necessary.

A mend is accomplished by pointing the rod at the fly, lifting the rod a little to get the line off the water, and then, in the same motion, rotating the wrist in the direction you want the line to go. If the motion has the proper snap to it, it will force the rod tip into a quick little roll that will be transmitted down the fly line, forcing a loop of line to hop off the water. If you want to make a bigger loop, make the motion bigger and slower. If you are a beginner and have never done this, you'll find it is easier to execute than I have made it sound. The trick is to perform the mend without affecting the drift of the fly. But don't panic if the fly gets jostled; even the best anglers do that. Some rods mend better than others, and thinner fly lines are easier to mend than thicker ones.

When fishing upstream, take up slack at a pace fast enough so the fly line doesn't loop below the rod tip. Most anglers are much too lax about slack line. When it gets excessive, drag is increased, and strikes are missed. In really fast water it is a lot of work to keep ahead of charging line. You can stay ahead in the race by pulling in long sweeps, starting as soon as the fly hits the water. Many anglers' strips are too short and jerky, and that doesn't get the job done. Make the first and all subsequent sweeps long and smooth.

When you are fishing upstream into a pool that spills out very quickly at the tail, try to be close enough for your rod tip to reach over the pool itself. If you are too far back, the line catches in the fast current that's breaking over the lip of the pool; it will grab the line and drag the fly. It may be impossible to get close enough to get into ideal position, but you may be able to lay your line over a rock to keep it from dragging. By moving a step to your right or left, you can have your line fall on a rock, where the current can't get ahold of it.

If angler moves to his right, line would lay on rock (x) and not be sucked out of pool. Credit Wes Edling.

Although a mend is often a good idea at the very end of a float, just before a fly is going to drag, reaching way out with the rod is a better choice. You avoid a difficult mend, and you're in a much better position to set the hook should your fly be attacked.

Chapter 10

FLIES

Because I've been "forced" to tie thousands of flies I have great respect for the art exhibited in a finely tied fly—but I must also confess that years on the water have left me a nonbeliever concerning the "mystique" surrounding fly patterns. I've had countless occasions when a companion and I have fished in different directions, and at the end of the day we found that we had about the same amount of luck but on totally different flies. When you're in the thick of catching fish you'd swear that the fly was the secret for your success; more likely, the fish simply started feeding when you attached Mr. Lucky Fly to the leader.

Can changing flies make a difference? Sometimes—although if the fish aren't feeding, they aren't feeding.

Mr. Lucky is then his owner's favorite fly—until it is dethroned by another pattern that finds its way onto the leader on another fortuitous occasion. Personally, I've had a hundred "favorite flies" that have gone in and out of fashion.

Almost every fly fisher I've ever met is under the illusion that changing flies will make the fish eat. My clients are forever saying, "Why don't we try something different?" I, too, always hope that the next fly is going to do it, though my experience would have me say, "No sense changing flies because the fish aren't feeding."

Choosing the Right Dry Fly

My simplistic approach to fly choice is in part due to the fact that I usually fish for stupid trout in relatively remote areas. When trout are hounded and/or are feeding on a particular food, they may require considerable head scratching. But choosing the right fly is not really that complicated. For instance, a Parachute Adams in an appropriate size will imitate almost all mayflies, and by changing to another body color, it would imitate *all* mayflies. Fish on flat water can be really particular, and if that's the case, you can give them a Comparadun (no hackle flies). That dry fly will fool most any difficult trout, but not necessarily the first time they see it.

Look Through the Trout's Eyes

Both the Parachute Adams and Comparaduns ride with their bodies flush on the water. That style of fly is easy for the fish to examine, so it must present the proper silhouette. When I'm tying dries I check the all-important silhouette by holding the fly above me at arm's length, toward the sky, and then examine it with squinted eyes. This is not a highly scientific approach, and might be based on a wrong assumption, but this is how I suspect a trout sees a fly. A dry that imitates a mayfly should have a thin body that tapers from thick toward the eye to thin by the tail.

With a caddis the body should be tapered in the other direction, but, more importantly, a caddis's wing needs to be tent style over the body. Many commercial grasshopper patterns are tied out of proportion. A natural grasshopper is a fat bug, and many hopper imitations are simply too skinny.

You've Got to See Them

Of course, a big consideration with dry flies is their visibility. As my eyes grow weaker I choose more and more dry flies with bright wings. The old standard white wing on a dry fly is not as visible as bright lime green or orange. Even big dries like the Chernobyl Ant can be surprisingly hard to spot too, so it wise to have some bright wing material that projects skyward on them.

Easy to Tie, Effective to Use Nymph

I might get run out of town for confessing this, but I fish one nymph pattern 80 percent of the time. My "favorite fly" is an ugly rascal, but very easy to tie. It was born of noble birth as a full-fledged bead-head Gold-Ribbed Hare's Ear Nymph. But I have reduced it to such an extent that I hate to embarrass the famous pattern by continuing to call it by its given name. Actually I can't take credit for the development of this fly—the "reductions" were the fishes' doing—or should I say their undoing. Because they were so fond of the original, their enthusiasm stripped it of its tail and hackle. If the fish were going to amputate those appendages and continue to attack the fly at the same lustful rate, I told myself, why should I bother tying all the stuff on in the first place? Then the gold ribbing got ensnared in some of the trouts' teeth, and the fly still caught fish. So it seemed to me that that accoutrement could be deleted as well. What that leaves is some brown fur with a gold bead ahead of it. Smear it with super glue and, *voila*, the Shit Fly. I suspect that the fly could even go a step further—just gold bead on a hook without any help from the fur behind, but I'm not ready to be that blasphemous—just yet.

I tie them on short-shanked, wide-gap hooks because I then have a fly that imitates a No. 18 but has the gap of a 16. (A wide gap hook catches more fish than a narrower-gapped hook.) Because I like being able to just change flies instead of adding or subtracting weight, I tie them in a couple of different size beads.

The Good & Bad of Streamers

Unless my clients are after only big fish I seldom have them use streamers. It is an exciting type of fly to use because many fish are seen as they chase it. The problem is that often not that many of the trout actually take it. It is a great type of fly, however, for locating big trout. An effective strategy, especially if you are fishing with someone else, can help you outwit a dumb trout. If a big trout threatens your streamer but doesn't take, cast again and have your partner put a nymph "on his head." He may not be fooled by the streamer, but it may have inspired his appetite enough so that he gloms the nymph.

One thing I have noticed is that most anglers want to fish streamers that are too small. Fish of decent size are attracted to big food.

Last summer my son Nick and I were fishing a very remote stream in the southern Rockies. We were trading off fishing the creek and catching the ignorant browns at a brisk pace. When it was my turn to fish the next pool I hooked a 9-inch trout that got relocated at my all too vigorous strike. It came off the hook when it landed, yet a half second later it started jumping all over the place. Then Nick and I saw, to our amazement, a trout that was maybe 18 inches grab the 9-incher. It was like watching a snake eating something that is too big for it. The bigger fish became totally incapacitated at trying to swallow such a hearty meal. As they tumbled downriver we followed as the larger fish continued to consume the smaller. By the time they had drifted 50 yards downstream all that was left of the 9-incher was the tail sticking out the mouth of the bigger brown.

When choosing a streamer, remember that big fish prefer big meals.

I also recall seeing a brown trout of about 10 pounds in Argentina rush up and grab a 12-inch rainbow that I was in the process of landing. Big fish want big meals, and our streamers are too small. I just measured the biggest streamer in my fly box, and it was 2 inches long—just an appetizer for a grown-up brown trout.

Chapter 11

NYMPHS

A s emphasized in Chapter 8, "The Strike," anglers detect only a portion of their nymph strikes and then hook only a fraction of those fish. The quickest will hook 50 percent at best. Consequently, a nymph needs to be rigged and fished so that it not only attracts trout but also instantly signals their takes. Then it's up to the angler; the quicker his reaction time the more trout he will catch.

Strike Indicators

Some anglers don't like strike indicators. Many even find them aesthetically questionable. They are hard to cast, they do spook fish, and they often impede the natural drift of the fly, but very few fly fishers have ample focus and dexterity with the rod to not use them. I know only three: rod builder Bob Widgren, my brother Jackson, and my son Nick. They take up slack—just the slack, never pulling on the fly—by raising the rod as the fly drifts down toward them. They look for the line to tighten and set the hook when it does.

Those of us incapable of such concentration use bobbers. Strike indicators are our link with the underwater world and, as such, deserve attention here. First, no matter what type of indicator you use it needs to be properly placed on the leader. One common mistake that many fly fishers make is putting their indicators next to the fly line. The thickness of the leader, plus kinks and slack spots, make transmission of information between bobber and fly slow and unreliable. Always place the indicator as close to the fly as possible and move the indicator up or down the leader at the same time that you change weight for different depths and currents.

The flat, square, paste-on indicators will fit through the rod guides so that flies snagged in the river can be easily freed. I believe the best indicators, however, are the cloth type that can be tied on with a slip knot. They are very sensitive and send clear messages as to what's happening in the depths. The big, bobber-type indicators are great if you have to do a lot of mending. Using a large dry fly as an indicator has a similar effect.

When nymphing upstream, try to keep your indicator in the same current as your fly. When they are in different flows, there will be drag, or slack, between the two. Slack will prevent you from knowing when a fish takes because the creature will spit the fly out before the leader pulls tight against the indicator. This is

This fish will take and eject the fly and the angler won't know anything about it because of slack between indicator and fly.

actually a very common occurrence, and countless trout are missed because of it. Of course, it is best to fish in such a way that this doesn't happen. Avoiding slack isn't always possible, so if you're having that problem, try putting two indicators on your leader. If you space them a couple of feet apart, it will help you keep track of what is going on, and then keep excess slack from forming. Use different color paste-ons. For example, if a green one is upstream of a red, you know that things are flowing along in good order. If they are backward, something is awry.

Bothersome Curving Casts

Another somewhat common problem occurs when a nymph curves around when it's laid down. This happens when too forceful a cast "shocks" on the final stroke. The line comes tight, and a heavily weighted fly will *zing* around in a sharp curve. The drift will start out with slack. A fish may take, but you won't know anything about it. All that junk can be cast smoothly so that it lays out straight. It's done by taking the snap out of the final stroke and softening the delivery. It also helps to release a foot or two of line when the cast is landing. If the cast does hit the water with unwanted slack, pull on the line to straighten it out.

Deep-Water Nymphing

When nymphing in deep water, thin leader material will get a fly down much quicker than a thick tapered leader. Consequently, less weight is needed, and less weight makes for more natural drifts. If you fish a lot of deep, fast water, try this rig: Tie a 2- or 3-foot butt section of braided Dacron fly-line backing to the fly line; below the Dacron use several feet of 2X tippet, then tie on your standard terminal tippet down to the fly; you can place weight above the tippet knot, and the indicator can go near the Dacron-2X connection; use a substantial indicator—a real cork one, perhaps—that will act as a buoy. The supple Dacron can be

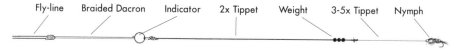

Deep-water nymph rig.

mended and moved this way and that without jostling the big, stable bobber. Long drifts, necessary in deep water, are then possible. This is, of course, an abominable setup to cast, so come way around in a circle when you sling it—and duck just in case.

If the fish are deep, be sure to cast far enough upstream of their suspected lie so that the fly has a chance to sink into position. Incidentally, this is usually farther than most anglers think. Be sure to use the right amount of weight. A really good nymph fisherman will change weight often, sometimes at each pool. How much weight? The rule of thumb is that the fly should touch bottom, or fish, occasionally. If you are hitting bottom all the time and getting snagged a lot, you are using too much weight. If your fly makes a few drifts without touching bottom, increase the weight.

Have a box of assorted small split shot and B shot—that's B, not BB—for deeper water. Clamp the shot above the tippet knot some 10 to 18 inches above the fly, so that it doesn't slide down. If the shot slides down to the fly, trout will avoid it. Soft lead works well in places where you want the fly to sink slowly, like in gradually deepening riffles. Lots of good fishermen use twist-on lead, but it is not my preference.

I used to think that the dry–dropper combo was best for just shallow water, but I have learned to run a heavy bead-head on several feet of tippet for deep water. Use a dry that is going to float no matter what, because if you use a dry fly that sinks, you will never be sure about strikes. Hoppers and stoneflies are great floaters and easy to see. A lot of fish, even sophisticated ones, will eat these juicy flies just for the hell of it, even when they are out of season. This "hopper-dropper" rig is the weapon of choice of guides almost everywhere. It seems to catch more fish than just a nymph with an indicator. This is partly due to the fact that the bobber (the dry) has a hook in it and catches fish, but the nymph produces more hookups, too, probably because of its close proximity to the dry. Because the dry is right above the nymph, it telegraphs the strike instantly.

Subtle Strikes

Although a telltale sign of a big fish taking a nymph is a very solid stop or sideways movement of the indicator, most strikes are subtle. So when that indicator bounces, stops, jiggles, shakes, twists, shimmies, dips, or dives, assume it's a fish and fire away at the least provocation. Often it's just the bottom, but if the fly is that deep, it is time to get it up and out of there anyway. Many of my clients don't react to a nudge on the indicator when their fly is drifting through shallow rocky spots because they think it is bottom, nor do they think a trout would be in such thin water. If that happens once, and doesn't happen on subsequent casts, you can be sure it was a fish. I'm always generous about pointing this out.

Remember, the Indicator Doesn't Have a Hook

The ever-so-intelligent trout sometimes shuns our cleverly tied flies and eats the strike indicator instead. They especially like orange. When this happens, your natural reaction is to set the hook. Because there is no hook in the indicator, ripping the thing out of its mouth will only spook the fish. If you can avoid striking, the fish may take the fly on the next cast.

Chapter 12

DRY-FLY FISHING

Seeing Is Believing

The first rule of thumb with dries is, whenever possible, use flies you can see. That means they have to float well, because if they sink, you can't see them. So when there are no flies on the water to guide your choice, start with the big, bright, and bushy. If fish come up for your large dry and make splashy rises, but you feel nothing when you set the hook, you are getting false strikes. False strikes occur when the trout changes its mind at the last second and its tail slaps the surface as it heads for home. When that happens, a smaller version of the same fly often does the trick. Which size dry you choose also depends on the time of the season. Insects tend to be larger, and trout dumber, at the beginning of the season.

The two-fly rig, made up of a very good floating dry and a bead-head nymph dropper, is standard fare these days, but not many anglers are familiar with the joys of fishing two dries. It's a great setup when the trout are taking something small and hard to see because you can put it behind a more visible fly. Tie the tail fly 3 feet behind the lead fly. The closer fly will absorb a lot of the drag, giving the tail fly a good float. When it is hard to see your smaller fly because of fast water or low light, use the hand fly as a locator. If anything "funny" happens near the hand fly, set the hook. Attaching a tiny piece of paste-on strike indicator 2 feet above a small dry can be helpful at times too. Of course, another advantage of fishing two flies is that it isn't long before you start seeing that one is preferred over the other. In that case, you may want to fish two of the preferred flies.

Dry-Fly Hotspots

All rivers have spots where fish are likely to be found rising when they are not coming up elsewhere. These are usually shallows, foam lines, places where currents sweep against bends, eddies, and natural funnels. There is no black-and-white description of these spots, but more food will be floating there than anywhere else. Quite often these spots are in a protected nook out of the prevailing winds, where insects are not swept away on the breeze. If you fish a section of river often, you get an intuitive feel for when fish will be rising in these places.

Skating in the Wind

Trout don't usually rise when it is windy because insects are unavailable if they are blown off the water, and the choppy surface makes them harder for the fish to see. If you love to fish dries, head to the river on calm and overcast days when insects are active and trout are not shy about rising.

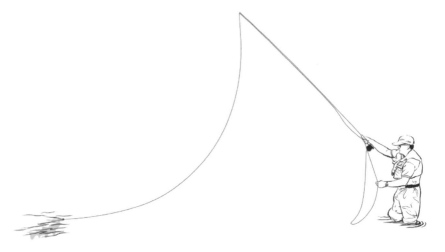

Skating dries is about as fun and exciting a way to fish as there is.

But at certain times it is smart and fun to skate dries on the wind. This is a marvelous way to fish caddis hatches, such as the Mother's Day hatch on the Rio Grande in New Mexico and on the Arkansas in Colorado. It is important to truly skate the fly in these situations, which means holding the rod high and fishing short, so that line and leader are in the air and only the fly is on the water. Use a 9-foot rod and a fly or two that are tied with stiff hackle and hair, such as the Solomon Hair-Wing Caddis. Because trout often miss the fly, skate it slow enough for them to catch it. Also, don't set the hook at the sight of the rise. Instead, watch the curve of the line and leader; when it tightens, set the hook.

Skating dries is especially effective in late evening, when fish are feeding on top. You may know this frustrating scenario: It is near dark, nice trout are rising everywhere, and you can't see your fly. Now is the time to use a trick I learned when I was a kid from famed Adirondacks guide Fran Betters. Take out your little flashlight and cut your leader back to where it gets thick—1X or so—and tie on a large dry. Then skate the fly over those hungry fish. When you hear, see, or feel something, set the hook. When the light gets that low and the fish are eating like mad, they throw caution to the wind, and the wisest old fish in the stream are easily fooled.

Fran and I used to pass over a certain bridge pool on the way to and from our own personal watering hole. We were usually in a hurry to get to our ultimate destination and consequently fished the bridge pool on the way home, when time meant little, it was dark, and we were a bit tipsy. We'd grab a rod out of the back of the car, cut the leader down to about a foot, and drag a huge dry across the surface of the pool below us. When we hooked one of those big bridge browns, we'd handline it up across the railing so as not to break the rod.

Skating dries is a great way to fish in windy Patagonia also. At the suggestion of master guide Jorge Trucco, I tie a dry pancora crab imitation and skate it. Jorge told me that large trout often chase pancora, a crayfish-like critter, to the surface, where they skip along in a panic. If you have seen some of those huge browns in the Argentine, you can understand the pancora's terror.

Don't Line Them

A big no-no in fishing for rising trout is lining them, that is, putting line or leader over the fish. Many people get excited and fire away when they see a trout coming up—and spook them. Take a few deep breaths and make a cast with a measured amount of line that you know is well short of the fish. Add a few inches at a time until your fly lands to your side of and just above the fish. Many anglers make the ugly mistake of letting go of the line and shooting it in such delicate situations, losing control of the distance of the cast and thus lining the fish.

Don't Be a Drag

Another common mistake is casting too far upstream of rising trout. By the time the fly reaches the fish, it's dragging. If you can learn to drop the fly right on the fish's head, it may eat it without thinking. Sometimes that's the only way to fool very selective fish.

Most fly fishers don't realize how often their fly is dragging. This is often because they are 30 or 40 feet away from it and can't see the little bit of drag—but the fish can. Trout often grab for dragging dry flies but miss them. I'm not sure whether they decide that the fly is acting unnaturally and miss it on purpose, or they misjudge it because of the drag and consequently hit behind it.

Under some circumstances it is best to present the fly from upstream of a rising fish. That is the preferred method for difficult, leader-shy trout in flat water. But making the perfect cast that drops the fly just right is difficult. Instead, cast beyond the current that your fly needs to be in, raise the rod, and pull the fly toward you. Once you have got it straight upstream of the riser, lower the

rod down, thereby sending the fly into
the fish's jaws. Of course, have
enough slack in the line so that the
fly reaches the fish without drag.
Add slack by shaking line out
of the rod. Do this by holding the rod close to the
water and waving it back
and forth.

Shake rod from
side to side while
feeding line.

Capitalize on the Hatch

When you run into a nice hatch, take advantage. Many hatches
only last for 15 minutes, so make them pay while you can. When
there are multiple hatches, fish take little breaks to digest and
stretch between meals.

Fast-Water Advice

The faster the water, the less ranging the trout will do to feed.
Because fish don't see the fly well in churning water, you should
cover such areas thoroughly. Another tip about fishing really fast
water with dries is to drop your fly just below the white water.
Fish aren't in the white stuff, and the fly will only get sunk and
lost there.

Sight Insights

When sight fishing, keep in mind that the closer a fish is to the
surface, the likelier it is to eat a dry. When you can see the body

This fish "felt" the plop of a hopper and swam 20 feet to get it.

of a rising trout, watch what it does when your fly goes over it. The more interest the fish shows, and the closer it comes to your fly, the closer you are to having the right imitation. Avoid putting the same fly over the fish repeatedly because if the fish sees the fly and doesn't take it, it will be unlikely to consume it on subsequent casts. A lot of activity only frightens the fish, so go ahead and change flies after just two or three good floats over the trout—or go find a dumber fish. If you stay with that trout though, take your time. If it stops rising, don't cast until it starts rising again.

When you are sight fishing with grasshoppers in slow water, be careful not to smack the big fly right on the fish's head. The great thing about a hopper is that fish feel the fly *plop* and will travel a good ways to take it. So, drop the fly a few feet to your side of the fish. Choose hoppers that will plop like a natural. I had a client who fished for a very long trout that was cruising under a grassy bank looking for hoppers in a shallow pool in Argentina. The fellow cast 20-plus feet short of the fish, and I was about to tell him to get it closer when, to our amazement, the trout turned toward the fly, casually swam straight at it, found it, and ate it. The best hopper fishing usually occurs in the late afternoon when it's warm and windy. Scattered clouds are helpful because trout are more prone to rise when there is some shade.

Keep Dries Dry and Buoyant

Wash and grease your fly after each fish. Drying crystals can be very helpful too.

Chapter 13

THE SWING

When I started fishing in Argentina I did what most of us *jan-kees* (Argentine pronunciation) do when we travel to a foreign destination: I did it my way. I worked hard wading against those big rivers, fishing dry flies and nymphs upstream as is customary here in the States. I caught fish in a lot of places, but on the big, wild rivers I saw that my Argentine friends were catching more fish than I—with less effort—by fishing downstream. They were swinging nymphs, Woolly Buggers, and other streamers on both floating and sink-tip lines.

Swinging a Woolly Bugger on a sink-tip line resulted in this fat brown.

I suspect that swinging flies works well where the trout eat stuff that swims—minnows, sculpins, crayfish, and the Argentine version of the latter, the pancora. Swinging is also a great way to fish when the water is high or the fish aren't feeding. That style of fishing seems to work best on gullible trout.

Swinging often produces a lot more action than fish because the fly interests trout that either don't eat or strike short behind the fly. But as a lot of water gets covered and a lot of fish get to see the fly plenty of them will end up caught.

Getting Into the Thing of Swings

What exactly is swinging? At first glance it seems like a simple matter: Merely cast across the current and hold on tight as the fly swings around with the current. Plenty of trout are hooked just that way too. But, as with all tactics, some folks catch a lot more fish doing this than others. The most successful learn to hang the fly over the fish. That is, they don't simply hold the fly in the current right below them, because that fools only small fish. Bigger trout like to grab the fly just as it is quartering downstream. The fish follow the fly across the current, and once it starts to slow they nail it. If the angler can maximize that brief window when the fly hangs suspended during that quartering action, he will hook more fish.

Let's imagine a cast across a moderately fast and even current. When the fly starts swinging across the stream, the line forms a wide belly. That loop increases as the fly crosses the river and by the time it is three-quarters of the way across the stream, it will zip along at such a rate that no fish will be able to catch it. That makes for a lot of short strikes. If, however, the fly swims back to your side of the river slower and hangs more in the current, it will catch lots more fish.

The angler can accomplish this by: Wading out a little farther; ending the cast so that the rod is angled out in the river, thereby lessening the angle at which the fly swims; and mending and lifting line upstream so that it doesn't "bow."

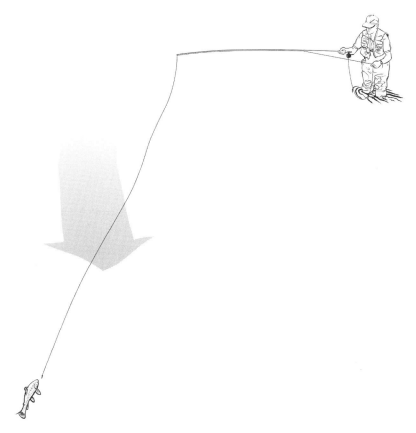

Hanging the fly in the "sweet spot."

Dance the One-Step

This type of fishing is designed to cover a lot of water. At the completion of each cast the angler should wade downriver a step. British salmon fishermen have been doing this for centuries, proceeding at an easy, even pace. It sounds simple—cast, step, then cast, step again—but it takes more attention than one might imagine. My clients miss the beat of this little jig more often than not.

A common blunder is forgetting to step. They'll make three or four casts from the same spot and then, when they realize they missed the beat, they take a couple of extra steps downstream to get back in rhythm. This concentrates the fly in one area and lessens their chances for action, because the best odds are laid when new water is fished on every cast. Fish that are willing to take a fly that is swinging will be aggressive and probably don't need a lot of looks anyway. Certainly some pieces of water deserve more attention than others, but, in general, if you have lots of river to fish, try to cover new water with each cast.

Chapter 14

THE FLY FISHER-MAN OR WOMAN

Most guides in the fly-fishing business will tell you that women are easier to teach than men. Women don't have as much tension in their arms—tension that is detrimental to fluid casting. Their egos aren't all bound up with being "top rod." I believe that it stems from the fact that they really don't care about "just fishing" and tend to enjoy nature more than men do. They'll even come right out and say, "I just like being here." This has been proven to me on many occasions, when a woman would actually put aside her rod and sit down to enjoy the wild world around her—while the fish were biting! When I've suggested that it might be better to become inactive when the fish are in a like frame of mind, they've usually replied, "You go ahead and catch a few." That is not a common male response. Here is a little story to illustrate the male and female mentalities.

Bluegills and Bobbers
On the drive to the stream Bill tells one fishing story after another. These aren't bluegill-and-bobber stories. They're fish tales of high adventure—salmon beyond the Iron Curtain, billfish on the high seas, and huge sea-run trout of Tierra del Fuego. As we four-wheel over a jumble of rocks and roots he talks about night fishing for the man-eating catfish of the Amazon. Wife Gloria is in the back looking out the window cool and disinterested, as if her husband's fishing stories have traveled this road before—through one ear and out the other. She volunteers something about their friends who fished at such

and such a lodge and that their son worked as a guide one summer. She's certainly not unhappy with this trip into the New Mexico wilderness; she just seems, well, along for the ride.

Our hike to the water takes us through a virgin forest, which seems to inspire wonder in Gloria. She interrupts an epic marlin battle to ask the name of a tall, flashy wildflower. I tell her it's fireweed. Encouraged, I take them a few feet out of the way to where a beaver is making slow but steady progress on a foultasting pine. The 3-foot-thick tree is gnawed about halfway through its trunk, and a crack that runs up the tree has formed. On the sway of each breeze the crack opens and closes as the giant moans its death song.

When we arrive at the stream, things look good. Mayflies are dancing up and down in shafts of light, and a couple of yellow Wilson's warblers flit about catching them. Bill glances at the surroundings and utters the gruesome phrase that strikes fear into the heart of every guide: "Just point me in the right direction. I can take care of myself." I give him a couple of flies and the tiny amount of instruction that I think he will accept, and take Gloria for her first fly-fishing lesson. When away from Bill she confesses that she is doing this for him, as if I couldn't already tell, and that she will try it but asks me to go easy on her. I tell her that teaching is hard work, and the less of it I have to do, the better.

She seems fairly bored with the 15-minute crash course in casting. Her attitude changes quickly, however, once she starts fishing, because she somehow manages to drop her first cast on a fish's head. With the 10-inch rainbow attached to her fly she emits screams, squeals, and giggles that echo off the canyon walls. She reels the trout right up to the end of the rod and is frantically grabbing for it. Of course, the 6-foot space between her hyperextended hand and the end of the 9-foot fly rod creates a comical problem. When I stop laughing I suggest that if she can't reach the thing, she'd better let out some line so that

As opposed to a lot of men, most women anglers take the time to take in their surroundings and enjoy themselves.

we could get at it. That is just the start of things. The little fishes are in such a reckless mood that she starts catching so many that it isn't long before I leave her on her own and go looking for the boss.

He is planted right where I had left him—and looking mighty out of place, zinging yards of line up the little brook. Any fish that might be interested in his fly—unlikely because it is dragging across several currents—would be thrown into a state of shock at the sight of his tall, well-postured figure towering over their home.

Before I have an opportunity to speak to him, his wife comes into view from downstream. She is now running on predatory instincts. We watch spellbound as she zeros in on her next victim. She creeps low to the edge of the stream, slithers behind a boulder, and waves her magic wand over the water. True, her cast is pitiful—limp-wristed and floppy—but it is perfect in the fast-falling stream because her fly settles on the water with plenty of slack, giving the fly a drag-free float. A wild slash of the rod and a loud shriek mean she has hooked another. Hubby's ears turn red as he slams a double haul to the next bend. This presents the perfect opportunity for me to do my job, and I try to suggest a more appropriate way for him to fish that little creek. He isn't too keen on making the "bad cast," and crawling is definitely beneath him, but before long he is slipping along the stream like a 10-year-old boy—and catching fish.

As we are preparing to leave he hooks what looks like the fish of the day, but it comes loose at the water's edge. He pounces down on the squiggling creature and pins it between his hands and knees. It pops out and into the drink. As this is catch-and-release fishing I am surprised to see Bill plunge in after the fleeing fish. After more squiggling, squirming, splashing, and crashing he raises the fish aloft for our admiration. The capture of that 14-incher seems to put the family hierarchy back in order, and he signals that it is time to go.

On the ride back Bill digs out a few more exotic fishing and hunting stories from far-off lands and waters. Gloria returns to her backseat position and adds, "That was fun. Let's do it again."

Teenagers have few preconceptions, and they learn quickly.

Chapter 15

KIDS

Kids have that famous knack for catching fish when they aren't supposed to be catching them. Years of study indicate no apparent rhyme or reason for these little miracles. A kid will have line wrapped around arms and legs one minute and be holding a wiggling trout the next. The fish gods favor the child.

Unless a child is very motivated, wait, then start them fly fishing when they are 11 or 12. I've noticed that many eager dads try to get their offspring fly fishing too early. The poor kids stumble and bumble about and get so frustrated that they get turned off to the sport. You might want to get them out there with the Snoopy Rod and bait first.

Kids are a pleasure to teach because their instincts haven't been crushed yet, and they can get into the flow quickly. I've seen some kids learn to fly-cast better in an hour than their parents have in a lifetime. I must say that I sink a little when I find out that a gifted, spontaneous child is heading toward a career in investment banking or some such colorful pursuit that will, in time, cut him or her off from his instinctive self.

Chapter 16

READING WATER

Anglers do better with guides than they do on their own because a guide has them fish only high-percentage spots. The average unguided angler pounds all the good-looking water. The guide, however, has learned from experience which places actually produce. Sure, other spots may hold plenty of trout, but that doesn't mean they are going to yield them. The currents may be too confusing, the depths too great, or perhaps the setup is such that the fish always see you coming. One thing all honey holes have in common is they all fish well. By that I mean these spots are situated so that a perfect approach and drift can be achieved.

Find Productive Spots
How can you—Joe Q Fly Fisherman—find these places? It isn't easy; in fact, it is, without question, the hardest aspect of fly fishing to learn. Hiring a guide helps teach you to identify good water because you will usually be standing in it. Later, when you are on your own, you can look for similar spots. When it all starts coming together, the light will click on and you will realize that certain sections of a river are much fishier than others. Obviously the best place to learn about water is on the river itself, but as you are currently limited to reading these words, here are some observations that may be of use.

Deep and Fast Water
An important thing to remember about deep and fast water is that the current is often much slower at the bottom than at the surface,

Reading currents can be confusing—but with experience, you'll learn how to interpret them quickly. Credit: Nick Streit

Although the water is raging at the surface, it may be much slower near the bottom, and harbor big trout.

and water that may appear to be too fast could actually hold some very good fish. Usually only large trout have the strength to inhabit heavy water. The problem is getting a fly down to them through the turbulence. Upstream nymphing is the method of choice because that style of fishing gets the fly down the deepest. The fly will likely take a different course each time in such wild water, and it may take many drifts before it actually passes in front of the fish, so make plenty of casts if the spot looks really fishy. Also, fish the heavy, deep water from a couple of different positions because the fly will do different things from each. Use a tippet long enough for the fly to get down, and if you aren't getting strikes, or touching bottom occasionally, add lead.

Undercut Banks

Look for big browns where the current has undercut earthen banks. Those slimy devils like working undercover. Such spots are especially favored in late summer when rivers are low, making hiding places scarce. The more lush the grass, the happier the fish will be because there will be more shade and terrestrial insects. These spots are good choices during bright sunlight when the trout feel more comfortable tucked away under something.

Most anglers don't realize how close their fly needs to be to the bank, and I'm forever saying, "Closer, get it in closer." The fish are under there for a reason, and they don't like to venture out very far to eat. The fly needs to float within inches of the bank.

The water is usually a bit slower right along the bank than out a foot or so, and getting a good float is not easy. If you are standing out in the main flow and casting in against the bank, the current you're standing in will drag your fly out of the slower current by the bank. Consequently, fishing the bank from the bank itself is usually best, and, as usual, the shorter the line you fish, the better the float. So get as close as possible, being sure to stand back from the bank a few feet so they don't see you, and walk softly so they don't hear you. This is especially important if the banks are soft and the current is slow.

Although the hopper-dropper rig is not easy to cast accurately toward the bank, it is otherwise perfect for this situation. The trout may be drawn to the hopper, but if it is dragging it will be refused. Trout will, however, tolerate more drag on a submerged fly than a dry, and they often grab the nymph after they refuse the hopper. On occasions when the fish take the dry over the nymph, remove the nymph for greater casting accuracy.

Slow-Water Strategies

Many anglers are seduced by the tranquility of slow pools. Despite their allure, these places are not usually very productive. If pools have fast water at their heads, that is where the fish will do the bulk of their feeding, because a greater volume of food lives and passes by them there. You can figure out where the trout are going to be in such fast water because there is character in the form of rocks, different-speed currents, and edges. You can read such water, but fish in slow water can't be located as easily, because their whereabouts are unknown in a featureless pool. Furthermore, because slow-water fish are constantly moving, if one does show itself, the rascal will probably be elsewhere by the time you get a cast to it.

Another concern in slow water is that trout have all the time in the world to inspect your fly to make sure they are getting the genuine article. Fast-water fish are easier to fool because they have to decide whether or not to eat quickly, before the meal washes away. Anglers also have an advantage in swift water because mistakes are masked by the water's turbulence.

A great way to fish quiet water is to team up with another angler. One of you spots the fish, and the other tries to catch them. That strategy requires a high bank that overlooks the water. One guy spots cruising trout from above and instructs the other as to where to cast. This can be productive, but the individual's fishing time is cut in half because politeness dictates that the spotter and the angler trade places. If you want to catch all the fish yourself, hire a guide and let him do all the spotting.

These slow pools are a favored location when the fish are rising, because you can easily spot trout and tell their size in flat water. This becomes particularly important when the light is bad, so when you expect a good evening hatch, make a plan that finds you in a long, slow pool at the end of the day. You'll be able to see both the fish and your fly much better than you will in fast water. When it gets so dark that you can't see much, don't stop fishing. That is when the big galoots turn reckless. The trick at that hour is to skate the fly and set the hook by sound and feel.

An angler wading close and reaching high with rod. Credit: Nick Streit.

Pick the Pockets

Boulder-strewn sections of river are great for the fly fisher who is willing and able to battle through them. Pocket water doesn't fish well from a distance, so aggressive wading is called for. Maneuvering streamers or wet flies through the pockets works sometimes, but you will usually do better by fishing flies on a dead drift. To get that effective natural drift, however, you have to be close—close enough so that the rod tip is over or near the pocket you are fishing.

This type of water tends to be of medium depth, so the hopper-dropper rig is usually the best choice. I like a dry stonefly on top, even in late summer after the hatch, with a bead-head nymph underneath it. If the pockets are short and deep, don't be shy about running 3 or 4 feet of tippet down to the nymph. Be sure the nymph has a heavy enough bead—this is where tungsten beads are great—to reach the fish.

Match Methods to the Water

It's a very good idea to choose methods of fishing that match the water in which you are fishing. Look at and think about the water you are planning to fish. If it is generally shallow, you might want to fish it with dry flies. The hopper-dropper shines in knee-deep water. If the water is deep, think heavy nymph. Woolly Buggers are great in tricky currents because they can be dead-drifted, sunk deep and jiggled, or maneuvered around rocks. Far too often I see anglers fishing in spots where they have little chance of success with the rig they are using. An example is fishing a shallow-running nymph in deep water. Some of my most successful days guiding are those when I carry a second rod that is rigged differently than the client's. That way we can fish two different types of water effectively.

What's It Worth?

When you start to get a fairly good idea of where the fish are, the next step is knowing how many casts each spot is worth. This depends not only on how many fish the place holds but also on how many casts it requires to fish it effectively. The really skilled angler may walk a half mile without ever making a cast and then throw a hundred times in one place.

Instinctive Fly Fishing

The final step of angling enlightenment comes when you find yourself hooking trout by gliding from pool to pool, without consciously following a selection process. When you have reached this stage, you've advanced—or is it reverted—to being an instinctive fly fisher.

Chapter 17

RIFFLES

Riffles can be characterized as fast, shallow water that runs over gravel and small rock. Since mayflies, caddis, and stonefly nymphs thrive in such locations, riffles are also where feeding fish congregate. Riffles that are connected to pronounced pools are best, because the deeper water of the pool provides protection from winter freeze-up, low water, and predators. Living is easy in such idyllic surroundings. The trout chill in the pool and then simply swim upriver when they get wind of a mayfly hatch. Riffles become even more important in rivers that suffer from heavy silt buildup because while the silt piles up in slower water, it is swept through the fast water of the riffle. Most insects do poorly in silt, and life is more concentrated in the riffles.

Make a Plan

Unlike other sections of a stream where structure may direct you to fish, many riffles have uniform, unbroken flows and consequently offer few telltale signs. Consequently, fish them systematically to cover this precious water. Most anglers just step in and fire away. Sure they may catch a fish or two, but if they had planned a strategy, they might have hooked many more. Stand on the bank for a moment and devise your plan. Most riffles are shallow at the head and deepen and slow as they descend. If you are fishing upstream with dries or nymphs, start just above the flat water, where the river starts to get shallow and has some movement. Work the riffle from right to left and, to avoid lining fish, make each cast a bit longer than the last. Never start with a

Angler standing in medium-speed, calf-deep water. There are many options here: He can fish the seams, he can fish pockets in the fast water, or he can fish the dropoff near boulder in foreground.

long cast and then make subsequently shorter casts. Assume that fish will travel a foot or two to grab the fly, and space your casts accordingly. Use a dense blanket of casts as you move up into the fastest water. The trout can't see well in the turbulence and may not see the fly unless it is very close to them nor will they move far to get it in fast water. Another reason to fish the heads of the riffles thoroughly is that the largest fish are often found there.

If the riffle is very large, fish it by *wading* back and forth across it a couple of times. I emphasized "wade" because if you physically move into position and cast straight upstream, you will get the best drift. (Actually the cast should be just a few feet to your right if you're a righty.) If you make long casts across the current and then mend, the drift will not be as true as the upstream drift.

Magic Current

Often you can find trout just about anywhere in a riffle, but a magic speed of current really attracts them. That favored water is usually below the really fast stuff, where the current begins to deepen and slow. A little surface chop that is a couple of inches high and dances this way and that typically characterizes such water. Plenty of food will be carried to the fish there, and they don't have to struggle against strong rapids to meet it. Also look for dropoffs near the head of the riffle because fish will sit in the slack water underneath the structure and grab food as it washes by them.

If a lot of food is washing down, the fish may get ravenous and move into very fast water to feed—or at least they may appear to be in very fast water. Actually, trout use tiny breaks in the current to escape the powerful head-on flow. When looking for these spots remember that even a big trout is only a few inches wide and the faintest break can hold a fish. In most rivers, though, it is rare to find fish in the really fast stuff. The lazy critters are much more likely to be found on the edge of the riffles— looking for that medium-speed current they love. When you

When approaching a large riffle, study it carefully, then map out a plan to cover all of the water.

Angler with good-sized brown. This current speed is ideal for big fish.

study a riffle be conscious of this because many are simply so fast that the fish are reduced to living on the edges.

If there isn't much edge, there won't be many fish.

Even if you are familiar with a riffle, check it out each time you fish it because changes in flow levels will dictate your quarry's position in the riffle. High flows push fish to the sides and lower flows move them into the middle.

Chapter 18

EDDY FISHING

Big trout do very well in eddies. It's an easy life: no fast water to battle; food conveniently circulating; and a blanket of foam providing overhead security. More importantly, trout are seldom removed from eddies because few fly fishermen know how to fish these great spots. Most anglers mindlessly throw straight casts into eddies from too far away, and the fly and line drag across the revolving currents and alarm the fish.

The Secret of Being Close

Eddies come in various shapes and sizes, so each requires an individual strategy, but most call for your getting close enough so that your rod tip is actually over the eddy. (The exception here is big eddies in large rivers.) Because the current along the bank is really running upstream, casting downriver to get a proper drift is necessary. Be careful, however, because fishing from the bank puts you up high where the fish may see you. Either kneel or hide behind something.

It is often possible to wade close to the eddy from midriver and then reach across the fast water to drop your fly from there. This is a good approach because it gives you a low profile. You can get much closer then you might suspect because trout seldom spook when fast water separates you from them.

Silt build-up is common in eddies so if you must stand in the revolving current of the eddy be careful not to send a warning of liquid dust ahead of you.

Try to place just your fly on the water—no line, no leader.

Fishing the Foam

When approaching an eddy that has a layer of foam on it, study the foam carefully because trout can often be found rising in the suds—even on days when fish are not coming up elsewhere. These fish, although often big, can be hard to spot because the food they are munching is usually dead, and only slight effort is needed for them to take spent insects in slow water. The rise of even a large fish may manifest itself as only a little nudge of the suds.

A few problems are inherent in presenting a dry fly in thick foam. One is that the foam and debris may muck up the fly. Another is that the fly may ride on top of the foam instead of flush at the surface, like the naturals do. In addition, the fish may have a hard time seeing your imitation in all that foam, in which case it is wise to get the fish's attention by slowly skating the fly over it. For the fly to look natural, the fly must be dragged over the fish *with no line or leader on the surface*. Obviously you must be very close to do this, but fish won't see you if the foam is thick. If the dry doesn't work, drag a lightly weighted nymph in front of the rising fish. As in any situation when fishing for rising trout, if

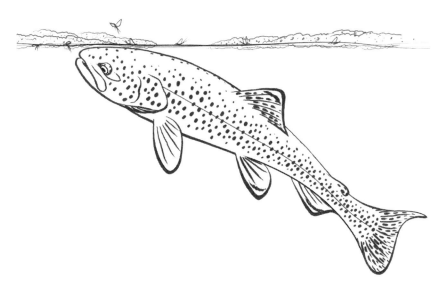

When you come to a foam eddy, watch it carefully before casting. Chances are a trout will be in there, feeding.

they stop coming up, stop fishing for them. If you stop fishing, the fish will usually begin rising again in a few minutes.

Get to the Bottom of Things

Eddies are often very deep, and the fish will not always be near the surface. The best way to get a fly down to them while maintaining the all-important dead drift is from the same close position you use with a dry fly. My brother Jackson Streit showed me this tactic: Take a heavy, bead-head Woolly Bugger and send it straight down into the depths. Do this by lowering the rod at the same rate that the fly is sinking. If you lower the rod too fast, slack will be created in your leader, and you won't feel a fish grab the fly. I have shown this technique to a thousand guided clients, and 90 percent of them will just flop the fly and leader down in a pile. At this point I want to scream because I know a huge trout is inhaling the fly—on a slack leader—and

Jigging an eddy can sometimes result in big fish.

there is no way for us to know anything about it topside. Practice lowering the fly in water where you can see it descend, and you will learn the proper pace. This is also a great way to fish other deep spots, such as undercut banks and deep swirling pockets.

Once the Woolly Bugger reaches bottom, jig it with the rod tip as it circulates the eddy. The fly will do its best work when it is straight down from the rod tip, and you may be able to walk it around the eddy if you think you won't spook the fish. When finished with the drift don't just yank the fly from the bottom to the top with a quick move. Give any fish that might be eyeing it a chance to eat by jiggling the tantalizing morsel all the way back to the surface at a slow, even pace. Try this maneuver for any predatory fish because lust often overtakes such impulsive creatures, and they grab the meal just as it is about to leave their domain. You can fish nymphs and streamers in these places too, but Woolly Buggers are wonderful teasers, with that sexy marabou swaying back and forth.

Chapter 19

STILL WATERS

Most guided clients prefer fishing moving water, and that's understandable because it is generally more interesting than pond or lake fishing. Still waters, however, offer a nice contrast to the chaos of moving water. And ponds are often at their best when rivers are unfishable, such as during spring runoff. Also, because the little fishies that live in still water don't have currents to battle, they grow more quickly into big fishies.

Fishing Pressure Matters

Fishing pressure is a critical issue on ponds and lakes because the fish can nose up to a fly and inspect it as if it were under a microscope. If they've been hooked in the recent past, the trout will be very difficult to fool. I have a couple of ponds that I use for guiding, and we try not to put too much pressure on them so the denizens don't get suspicious. If you don't have that option, and you find yourself fishing for difficult trout, use smaller flies, thinner tippets, and slow retrieves.

Read the Water

You can't read still water like you can a stream. Getting a good overview of a lake is helpful, and if a nearby hill provides a promontory, ascend it and look down for dropoffs, shallows, and other structure that will concentrate food and fish. If the lake is shallow, it will probably fish well with floating lines. Conversely if it is deep, plan to get down to them with sinking lines. Look for inlets and outlets, because they can prove to be key fishing

Inlets and outlets are always worth checking, as they're often productive.

spots. For example, if there is a good hatch in the feeder creek, fish will gang up at its mouth.

If the wind and light are conducive to good visibility, sight fishing is an exciting and productive way to fish. Look for elevated shorelines from which to fish, because it is easier to spot cruising trout if you are above them. If the fish is close to the surface, it may take a dry fly. If it's several feet deep, you may need to tie on a bead-head nymph and cast it far in front of the fish. The fly needs to be on a collision course with the trout because it usually won't come upward very far to take it. Don't move or watch the fly; look at the fish. If it is coming for the fly, it will speed up a little and change course. When you see the whites of its jaw open, set the hook. Use a single nymph in this situation and tie it to a long leader and tippet, so if the fish is deep, the fly will be free to sink quickly.

Of course, you can't very well sight-fish if you can't see fish. Some folks are better than others at spotting them. Always walk slowly and study the water carefully. Usually, feeding fish will be on the move, and that is the giveaway. If you think you see something that looks fishy, but you're not sure, cast to it quickly. Many times I see clients pondering whether they are seeing something—as the "something" swims away. After years of fishing I have learned to trust my initial instincts in these matters: If I think that I saw something, I probably did.

The fish love to cruise along shorelines and next to and over weed beds, so it may be a good idea to cast along this structure and retrieve a fly parallel to it. Although structure is not as important to trout as it is to bass, for example, they love the shade and will be found under trees. They are not there to ambush prey like a bass would be, but more because of the overhead protection and the food falling from the trees.

Using a dry fly–dropper combination is a great way to fish rivers, but that setup works well in still waters too. The trick is to have the nymph at the appropriate depth. That may range

Trolling from a tube can be a deadly tactic.

from a few inches to a few feet. In the rather common case of trout rising for emerging midges I like to put the little subsurface emerger only a foot behind a small dry. For example, a No. 16 Elk Hair Caddis with a light tan wing is very visible, and midging fish will often take it.

Fishing in a Tube

Fly fishing from tubes is easy living, maybe even downright lazy. Unfortunately, most folks don't get into the spirit of it and work their butts off by casting repeatedly. Whether fishing dry or wet flies you'll find it more productive to keep your fly in the water than in the air.

I have found it best to have my clients troll wet flies from the tube rather than cast them about randomly. (Unless they are casting at fish or some sort of quality structure.) Trolling is effective because the fly is always in the water, and your hands and rod are always in position to set the hook. And if you are fishing deep, your fly will be at that effective depth all the time. The alternative, constantly casting and retrieving, puts the fly in the air, sinking toward the proper depth, or rising away from it, keeping it where it belongs only half the time.

When fishing dry flies, cast to the area that the fish are working and don't move the fly. Sure, it gets boring to stare at a dry for minutes on end, but remember that the fish are on the hunt for something to eat, and they will eventually find your offering. When they do, it will be in a still, natural state. I find that the clients who are patient about this will outfish those who cast here and there.

It's a different story if the fish are rising nearby, and the angler holding the rod can cast accurately. Feeding trout are on the move, and the fly needs to be put on their head as soon as possible after the rise. I've noticed that most anglers are far too lackadaisical about this and don't realize the urgency of the situation. If the fish are actively rising, try keeping your line in the air with false casts. When a fish rises, fire away. The longer it takes to deliver the fly, the farther away the fish will be from its last known whereabouts. A big help is knowing which way the quarry is going after it rises. You can often tell by examining the ring of the rise. Rising fish push water ahead of them, and whichever way the wave is greatest is the direction the fish is heading.

Scout for Trout

Trout in lakes often patrol in circular patterns. If you can get yourself in a position to physically see fish cruising, you will get an idea of how fast and where they travel. Since their speed and patterns are fairly universal, your observations will help you outwit them in similar situations elsewhere.

In the last couple of years I have been wearing binoculars when fishing. They come in handy for many things, but their greatest use is for spotting rising fish. I'd often walked great distances to where I'd seen trout rising, only to discover when I got there that they were dinks. With the optics you can usually tell from afar if

This trout is headed left.

they are worth going after. Big fish leave bulky riseforms and tend to show body parts when they rise. They push the water in waves in front of them; the heavier the wave the heavier the fish. Another good use of the binoculars is looking for other anglers. See where they are fishing, and head the other way.

Chapter 20

HIRING A GUIDE

Hiring a guide is a great way to get around the nonsense of our apparently complicated sport of fly fishing and cut straight to the chase. You'll probably catch plenty of fish but, more importantly, you'll learn a lot. Of course, a guide can start beginners on the right foot, but people with moderate experience will benefit even more. Most have a head full of questions to be answered and bad casting and fishing habits to be corrected. Another angler who can be helped a lot is the city-bound fellow who endlessly reads scientific and technical books on fly fishing. Such experts are often in serious need of "de-education," and the experienced guide will help them sort through the jumble of info to point out what really matters. Such an overqualified angler will walk away from the river freed of the burden of insignificant details.

Find the Right Guide

However, you need a wise guide for this chore. How do you find such a reclusive varmint? You can check chambers of commerce, state game and fish offices, the Web, fly shops, telephone directories and so on. This will get you a list from which to choose, but remember that great fishermen are like artists: The best are seldom good businessmen and self-promoters, and thus may be hard to find—or have all the business they can handle. Call your fishing friends or acquaintances near where you are going. It won't matter whether they fish or not; they have probably heard the name of the best guide in town.

The author being inducted into the Freshwater Fishing Hall of Fame. He is flanked by author John Nichols (left) and Elmer Guerri (right).

Once you have identified your wily guide, consider your options before contacting him. First off, don't shoot yourself in the foot by limiting your options—"I want to fish a meadow stream for big fish, with dry flies, of course. I picture a tall tree on the left bank with some high peaks in the background...." Your poor guide will have racked his little brain all night thinking of an appropriate place to take you, and he—or she—won't be of much use come daylight. It is okay to suggest the type of fishing you would like, as broadly as possible, but try not to get too specific. Say that you want to learn as much as possible, catch a few fish, and have a pleasant day. This will ground your neurotic guide and give him sufficient choices to ensure a successful day's outing.

Maximize the Experience

When you get to the water remember that most angling guides are control freaks who get frustrated by witnessing bad fishing and casting. We never know how folks are going to respond to suggestions, so by all means solicit help. I always breathe a sigh of relief when my client says, "Feel free to tell me when I'm doing something wrong."

Be careful not to paint yourself into a corner with your guide. Many times on the phone or in the car a guy goes on about all the places he has fished and all the great fish he has conquered. At water's edge, however, it may be found that mighty Captain Ahab can't cast past his shoe, making for a most awkward situation. Just how are you going to tell a big-game fisherman that he has to practice his ten-to-two casting? We see very few really good fly fishers, so don't worry about sounding inexperienced. Once on the water you can't fake it anyway.

What's really important for the guide to know before the trip is your conditioning and abilities. This will allow him to match you with the water that suits you best. His figuring out your age, health, and skill over the phone is tricky business, so volunteer as much relevant information about yourself as possible. Then the guide has to apply geographical handicaps to the descriptions he gets. What might be a long hike or challenging fishing to some is a walk in the park to others. Westerners are used to covering a lot more ground on foot than Easterners. And what constitutes fly-fishing expertise changes from East to West, too. Easterners can do surprisingly well in the West because they usually have a lot of experience. Many have streams out their back doors and compete with their neighbors every evening to catch sophisticated trout. Eastern fishermen's greatest shortcoming is that when they get in the wide-open spaces of the West they usually poke along and don't cover enough water.

Unfortunately, those who might benefit the most from a local guide don't hire them. These are folks who have been fishing an area for some time, taking what they consider to be good catches. There is a big difference, however, between fishing for fun and fishing professionally, and the local sportsman might have quite an eye-opening experience by fishing with an accomplished guide.

I feel I have had enough difficult jobs in my life to qualify as an expert on that four-letter word, "work." I've roughnecked in the oilfields, fought forest fires, made adobes, built houses, surveyed, retailed, and spent long, snowbound winters tying thousands of flies. Guiding, when done well, is physically, mentally, and emotionally the most draining of the lot. The job consists of long hours of being an expert, therapist, sage, valet, cook, historian, and babysitter. Yet, since the guide is perceived to be a guy "who gets paid to go fishing," the world offers little sympathy. Of course, the perks include making people laugh under the open sky and never tiring of seeing fish inhale a fly. The absolutely best guides don't care who is holding the rod when it happens. That's the guide for whom you're looking.

Chapter 21

ADVICE FOR GUIDES

Start on the Right Foot

• Be on time. In fact, show up a few minutes early so that you can find out from the lodge owner about the trip, including what water is available, before greeting the clients. Then inventory their gear, outfit them, and get them out the door.

• Have everything you need so that you needn't make any stops once you're on the road.

• Have a relatively clean vehicle and clean windows.

• When deciding about where to go, ask the clients what they are looking for, that is, instruction, big fish, scenic places, few people, and so on. Remember that they are paying, and we need to do what they want, not what the guide wants.

• If a hike is required, be sure to check the folks out and carefully explain as accurately as possible "what getting in and out of the canyon is like." I can't remember the number of clients who have said, "Just take me anywhere. I don't mind the walk," then complained afterward about what a grueling trip it was. I have learned not to make a decision about where to fish until I lay eyes on the client.

• If it's one of those trips where the wife doesn't want to fish very much, believe her; she probably doesn't! Let her sit on the bank and be happy. She'll fish when she feels like it.

• When choosing a river or section of river, ask if they are right- or left-handed, because different sections of river may fish better for one or the other.

If a hike is required, a good guide makes sure his client is in good shape before heading off into the hills.

•Keep in mind that the client—not you—has the rod in his hands, and although you could catch a sack full of fish in one place, he might be blanked and very frustrated by the experience.

•Try to fish beginners and weak casters in fast water where you can get right up on the fish.

•When you have two or three sports, fish them together and leapfrog from pool to pool. Canyon-type creeks may not lend themselves to such a plan, however, because the fish may be spooked by someone forced to walk close to the water because the canyon doesn't provide room for someone to skirt the stream. In most situations, though, when you have folks close together, you can stay in control and move them as necessary.

•Never let one jackrabbit of a client get ahead of another. You will have lost control of where he is fishing and have no idea what water he has trashed for the other client. Think of the clients as cows that need to always be in green pastures. Don't let any wander off, but when herding them, be careful.

Herding Hints

•Be polite! If done right, guiding is a lot of work and can be very frustrating. I have been out with guides who were cranky; their disposition ruined the day. I've been accused of being a jerk to clients, and I can tell you that I am better off sitting on the bank for a few minutes and cooling off rather than losing it. Remember, rude is hell on tips.

•When guiding two or three anglers in small creeks you might want to fish only one or two at a time. This is even more judicious if the clients are interested in an "instructional" day.

•Beginners and Easterners love to dally around in one pool

forever, and success is usually much higher if you can herd them onward and cover more water.

Teach with Instruction and Example

- Give casting instructions if you are capable at it. If you are a self-taught caster who has never had professional casting lessons, you're probably not competent to teach.
- Start the day by fishing for three or four minutes. That way you give the client a picture of what you will be trying to accomplish. Start in a honey hole where you can easily catch a fish, proving that fish are in the stream, they can be caught, and that you are capable of catching them.
- Don't fish, except to demonstrate a point. Clients will never gripe about the guide fishing, but trust me, neither they nor the boss likes it. If it's been a long day, and the client wants to fish in the evening, it may be okay for you to fish—if you have already done a day's work and you have squared it with your client. With the right client it can be okay for you to fish the tough spots that they can't fish, but be careful: Your tip is pending. If "the John" asks you to fish, go ahead, but don't go crazy and run off upstream on the guy. Fish with him and try not to outfish him too badly. Remember: Your tip is pending.
- Carry a rod so that you can have it rigged with something different for different situations.
- Always carry an extra rod into the canyons because of the possibility of breakage.
- When fishing more than one person, try to have them catch an equal number of fish.
- The "expert" is usually the toughest client because he often thinks he doesn't need help. This is a very sensitive situation, so tread lightly because you don't want to bruise his ego. Say things, like "from my experience" or "last week when we fished this pool we stood just here and caught a huge one."

Lunch

Lunch is an all-important time. It's a good excuse to get away from the client and reorganize. One of the main problems with lunchtime is that it often coincides with the best fishing. So carry a snack and eat late if that is advantageous, for fishing often dies by 3 or 4 P.M.

Being a good fisherman is certainly an important part of being a good guide, but common sense, good manners, and an ability to teach are as important. Be honest about your experience—well, fairly honest—and if you find yourself getting frantic and obsessed, try to remember what I tend to forget: "It's just fishing."

Chapter 22

FIGHTING FISH

After watching people fight thousands of fish each year, you get an idea of why some land them—and why some don't. I can't do much to prepare people for fighting big fish. Sure, I can tie an old boot onto their line and throw it into moving water to illustrate the mechanics of fighting fish, but that still doesn't address the main problem.

Keeping Your Cool Is the Challenge

That problem is that anglers lose their cool. Often an angler doesn't have any cool to begin with and breaks off his prize when its instantaneous run triggers the fisherman's not-so-instantaneous response. At this critical point, the angler might freeze, clamp down on the line, heave, trip over his own feet, fall, flounder, scream and, sadly in extreme cases, drown. The size of the fish that causes such a state of insanity varies from one angler to the next. The beginning fly fisher may come apart with any size fish, but it may take a trophy of rare proportions to unnerve a seasoned angler. Rest assured that no matter how cool the customer, there's a fish out there that will rattle him. It's why we fish, isn't it?

Delightfully, the best way to learn how to overcome this affliction is by getting in the ring and duking it out with the lunkers. A bruiser at the other end of the line gets a lot more attention than an old boot, and the learning curve is steep when the stakes are high. Just one day with a good guide on a river like New Mexico's San Juan or central Oregon's Deschutes, for example, will teach you a great deal about fighting big trout.

When fighting a fish, try to keep your cool, no matter how large that trout might be.

Prepare for the Big Fish

You can do a few simple things to prepare for hooking and fighting Mr. or Mrs. Big.

- When in big-fish country, check leaders for wind knots and abrasions and never, never leave wind knots. They decrease the strength of your leader by half. If you check for wind knots often, you may be able to undo them before they become too tight to untie. Once they become that tight, the leader is comprimised, and you should cut off and replace the tippet.
- Check to make sure that hooks are sharp and not bent. If a hook is out of shape, don't try to bend it back. Discard and replace the fly.
- Before fishing a likely spot, examine the proposed battleground in case you should hook "The Big." Be aware of snags, routes downstream, and places to beach a monster.

•Don't fish with excess line hanging out of your reel. Use just the amount you need so you won't have a lot of slack to deal with if you hook a big one. Loose line has a habit of wandering around rod butts, reel handles, and other appendages.

Use Your Drag

After the fish is on, it is important to get it on the reel's drag system. This is a critical point in the fight. If you loop the line between the middle and fourth fingers, you can keep tension on each end while reeling in. This gives you a loop that can be watched and maneuvered as line is reeled in. This process does, however, require considerable dexterity with the fingers and is a tough operation for the inexperienced fly fisher to perform. Often a fish will be accommodating by running off with the slack. You can augment this, if you have done your scouting and know what's behind you, by backing up. If you start at midstream, backing up can put you where you need to be, that is, on the bank and in position to follow the fish downstream. If you reach the shore with the fish on the reel, you've won half the battle.

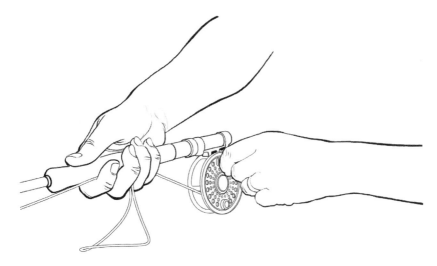

A dangerous time. Try to get your fingers away from the line a.s.a.p. when hooked to a lunker.

If you tend to break fish off just after striking, you may not be getting your finger off the line fast enough after setting the hook.

Fish break off when screaming reel handles come in contact with clothes and hands, so keep the reel out away from your body. If your reel has a good drag, don't even touch it until it's time to wind line in.

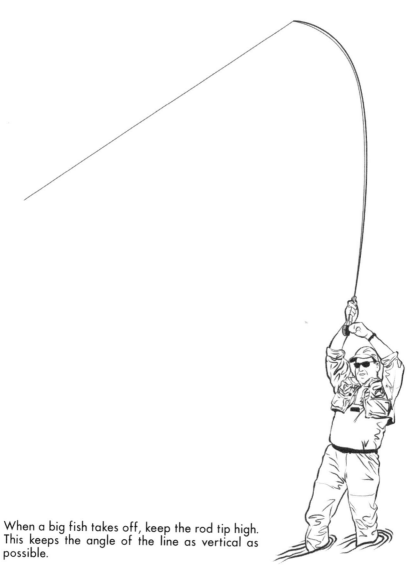

When a big fish takes off, keep the rod tip high. This keeps the angle of the line as vertical as possible.

When a good fish is hooked, anglers are often too cavalier about the event. Focus on the fight. Stay on top of the fish and keep your arms way up in the air. This is more important than people realize because it keeps the angle of the line as vertical as possible so there is less chance of getting fouled on the bottom.

There's a Place for Brute Strength
When a fish heads for a snag, you may have to apply real muscle to turn it. Anglers give too much credit to a fish by thinking it heads for a snag so that it can wrap the leader around it. The creature is merely scared to death and looking for a hiding place. For mathematical reasons beyond my understanding, a fly rod has much more power held sideways than overhead. To steer a fish, turn the rod in the direction opposite to that in which it is swimming. If the fish is going right, the rod should be horizontal and on your left side.

Apply maximum pressure, but only experience teaches you how much that is. Furthermore, though guides go nuts to see fish fought forever, beginners should go easy if conditions allow. I have seen a multitude of fish lost because the fisherman had no idea how much pressure to apply. You can put a lot of steady pressure on monofilament. The sudden stresses are what "pop" the line.

A fly rod has a lot of power when held to the side. If a fish tries to run to the right, hold your rod sideways to the left, and vice versa.

Net big fish by leading them in your net.

Keep Your Distance—But Keep Up

It is best to fight fish from a distance so that there is plenty of forgiving stretch available in the line and leader. And keep some distance between you and a green fish because the fish may freak when it sees you at close range, and make a wild dash, and break off.

A fly may pull out or break off if a heavy fish gets into the current and you don't follow it downriver fast enough. Always try to stay abreast of a large fish in a strong current so that you are not fighting it and the current too. The fish's weight is greatly increased by the added force of the current.

Concluding the Fight

Once the quarry has grown tired, you need to get its head above water and keep it there. This is when you finally have control, so don't ease up. Keep the fish coming at you and try not to let it get its head back under the surface. With its head above water, it can either be beached or netted.

Beaching a large fish works well if gravel bars or gently sloping shores are nearby. If the banks are steep or you are in the middle of a large river, a net will save you many fish. The shape of the net is important. Buy a net with a wide front rim so that you have room for error when you slide it under your treasure.

Chapter 23

WADING

The most successful fly fishermen work hard at getting close to the water they want to fish. Whether the objective is getting to a turbulent spot in the middle of a crashing river or slipping toward a riser in a quiet pool, wading is an important part of trout fishing.

Dress Right

For most rivers you need chest waders and spiked wading shoes. Spiked shoes take some getting used to because they skid on dry rocks more than felt-soled shoes do, but they really are great on round, slippery rocks. Not surprisingly, however, spiked shoes are unpopular with boatmen.

Gore-Tex breathable waders are marvelous, making neoprene waders passé. Neoprenes are okay for cold water, but breathable waders with sufficient undergarments are better. When the weather is warm, but not hot, I like to wear the Gore-Tex with nothing underneath. Many fly fishermen I guide—yes, we men are the stubborn sex—insist upon wearing waders on hot days when they would be better off without them. Often during summer I hear, at the end of long hike, "I'm hot. I wish I had taken your advice and waded wet." The main drawback of getting wet is getting cold, so bring extra clothes in case the weather changes. Wear neoprene socks, quick-drying pants, and no underwear (like jeans, underwear takes forever to dry).

I fish a lot of clients who don't use gravel guards, or gaiters, over their waders. These accoutrements keep gravel out of shoes. Gravel causes holes to wear in the wader feet and makes for uncomfortable walking. Gravel guards also keep shoelaces from coming undone and flies and line from getting tangled in the laces.

Staff Up

Wading staffs are handy tools, although they can get in the way while fishing. The kind that collapse seem to be best because they can be stashed out of the way when not in use. The low-budget angler can go to a ski slope (or ski shop) and find a lonely ski pole that has lost its mate, then turn it into a wading staff by simply tying a string to it. You can cut the cup off the bottom if you like, but leave it on if you typically wade in silted water. The only problem with metal staffs is that they make an unnatural sound when they strike a rock, and for that reason wooden staffs are better. I don't carry a staff, but when I have a hairy crossing to make I hunt one up on the way to the river. When I've made my crossing, I leave it on the bank for the trip back.

Tips for Troubled Waters

Here is one little trick that has saved me many a dunking. When in a hairy spot, tottering and about to go for a swim, slap your rod in the river and use its leverage against the current to stabilize yourself. You can put your rod in the river to keep your balance well before you get into trouble. I'm not suggesting you use the rod as a wading staff. Don't touch the bottom with it; just hold it in the current. I must admit, however, that I have stuck the butt end on the bottom and used it as a staff in emergencies.

Always wade facing upstream and never cross your legs. Don't let fear get the best of you. If panic tells you to dash for safety, stay put. Take a few deep breaths and continue slowly. Always wade slowly when in a tough spot.

When wading treacherous water with other people, link your arms or place your arms around each other's shoulders or waists.

Sticking your rod in the water can help you maintain your balance while wading. Credit: Nick Streit.

Rest assured that when your guide suggests such a union, he or she is not getting fresh but just trying to keep everybody dry.

Stealth Is Important

Wading quietly, without pushing a wake ahead of you, can be very important in many types of fly fishing. Wade slow, shallow water quietly because all fish are spooky in skinny water. An added problem occurs in streams with loose rocks. This is a real concern in Argentina because most rivers there run over soft-ball-sized round rocks that roll easily. When those rocks clink together, fish split the scene. The secret to quiet wading is taking smooth, even steps as you walk through the water. Avoid splashes or abrupt movements. Furthermore, don't false cast while wading delicate water; that creates disturbances too.

Another little trick about wading is to not fight the current unless you have to. When making a crossing, start as far upstream as possible and angle downriver with the flow.

When wading treacherous water, linking arms with a companion can help prevent a spill.

Chapter 24

SNAGGED

A few tricks can help prevent you from having to physically unhook a snagged fly. The benefit of getting unstuck from afar, besides saving you a walk, is that you're less likely to spook the fish between you and the errant fly.

Various snags hold onto flies differently. A fly hooked to a submerged rock will usually let go if it is pulled from the opposite direction from which it was hooked. This is very common when fishing upstream because flies get lodged between rocks. When you walk or reach around to free it, let the line loose. If you keep it tight as you go around, it has a tendency to stay hooked.

If you are hooked to a rock that is above the surface, a roll cast pulls the fly from the other direction, and the fly will come free four out of five times. This maneuver, however, seldom works when flies are hooked to submerged rocks or wood.

Releasing flies from wood is difficult because the hook is embedded in the material, and it becomes necessary to physically unhook the fly. This, however, can often be done with the rod. Recently I was fishing to a crowd of rising fish when I hooked a stick on the edge of the pool. I would have spooked every fish had I gone all the way down to the snag to unhook the fly by hand. Instead, I sneaked up to within 12 feet—the length of my arm and rod—and ran the rod tip right down on the snag. I then pulled the fly up tight to the tiptop eye by taking up the entire leader into the rod. A little jiggle and push in the other direction, and the fly was free. The fish thought the brown rod was just

Slide the tip top over the embedded fly, hold the line tight, and push. Credit: Wes Edling.

another stick and kept rising. I dried the fly off and caught a 17-inch brown on the next cast.

This handy trick saves flies and soaked shirt sleeves, too. It is especially helpful when nymphing snag-infested waters. Most strike indicators won't fit through the guides, however, so use flat roll-on ones that will. Although this technique might seem dangerous duty for your rod tip, I have never seen a rod broken when used this way.

Whether beginner or expert, we all hook many a tree. I supply flies when guiding, and since I hate tying the things, I equally disdain decorating the forest with them. Consequently, I have become quite the expert on the holding qualities of various plants, for the severity of the snag is dependent on the species of tree that has attracted the fly. When hooked to a pine, spruce, or fir high overhead, I usually just break it off without tricks or ceremony. Those trees don't like to let go, although ponderosas are more amenable to catch and release. When your fly lands in a softwood, it has a decent chance of coming out if you don't pull it up snug. Instead, snap, snap, snap with sharp little jerks. If you are hooked to a dead branch, snap it repeatedly at a right angle to the branch. The branch has a better chance of breaking when yanked on from that direction.

When snagged with sinking lines, try pointing the rod straight at the fly, then take the line in your hand and pull. When just shy of the breaking point, let go. The line will spring forward enough to pull the fly from the other direction—and sometimes let go.

.

Chapter 25

GEAR

Modern fishing vests have too many pockets, allowing people to carry a lot more than they need and causing them to fish more in their vests than in the water. Treat your supplies as a backpacker would: When in doubt, leave it out.

Close to the Vest

I have clients who fish far less than I do, but they carry a lot more gear than I. I'm guiding every day, and this is the list of what I carry: flies; floatant; tippet; leaders; weight; strike indicators; nippers; tiny Swiss Army knife (featuring scissors); needle-nose pliers; and a catch-and-release tool. Those are the fishing-related items.

Then there are the nonfishing items, which vary with conditions and locale: lighter; sunblock; spare lip gloss; tiny flashlight with extra batteries; adhesive bandages; a flat of duct tape; Super Glue; and drinking water.

Some optional items are a tape measure, binoculars, camera, and net.

What's Your Line?

Double-taper fly lines are better choices for most trout fishing than weight-forward lines because the thicker line of the DT feels better in the hands and doesn't tangle like the thinner WF lines will. For many trout fishing situations, 30 or 40 feet is a very important distance. With a WF line you don't have enough line weight in the air to load the rod well. And you end up having to haul or shoot line, blowing your accuracy.

Fly rods are our most important tool. Make sure you choose one that's right for the job and right for your casting style. Credit: Nick Streit.

Most Important Tool

Fly rods are our most important tool. For many anglers, their love of fine fly rods is their undoing because they have too many rods and don't fish with them often enough to be familiar with each one's personality. If you're not a great caster, it may be better to get to know one good rod really well. Make it the right rod for the job. Light rods are great for small dry flies, but outsmarting trout is sufficient challenge without imposing the additional handicap of being undergunned.

Rods less than 8 feet in length may be best for small brushy creeks. But long rods have merit also, because they allow you to reach out and dabble the fly. When shopping for a rod, remember that a 9-foot rod must be high quality; a cheap 9-footer may carry a light price tag but be heavy. Of the new top-of-the-line models, the 4-weights are probably the best all-round trout rods.

What kind of fly-rod action is best? My notes reveal that stiff rods catch more trout than soft ones because they tend to be accurate for short-yardage casts, and mend well. They throw the tight loop necessary to slice through the wind, and that tight loop will slip a fly under brush better than a softer rod. Of most importance perhaps is that stiff rods respond faster when a quick strike is needed when nymphing. Many anglers have a fast enough motion, but their rods react too slowly and give the fish just enough time to spit the fly out. Furthermore, when you are fighting large fish a stiff rod will give you more control over the fish and tire it out quickly.

Soft rods are great for midrange fishing of 30 to 40 feet. They are also excellent when you are using small flies on light leaders, especially when big fish are the target. They are better for casting two flies or weighted flies with strike indicators, because the wider loop soft rods throw keeps things from tangling.

Nets

While attending the Fly Tackle Dealer Show I noticed that the fad of the long, thin net seems to be fading. That's good news for the fish because these "catch and release" nets aren't as environmentally sound as their manufacturers suggest. By the time you fit, fuss, and finagle a trout into one of them, the fish might die of old age. Carry the biggest net that you can and be sure that it has a wide front rim.

Chapters 26
CATCH AND RELEASE

Not only do catch-and-release regulations ensure a continued supply of big fish, but they also help maintain nature's balance. If trout aren't removed from the system, the equilibrium among food, space, and cover stays stable, thereby maximizing a river's potential and creating hungry fish and happy fishermen.

I return fish for practical reasons: I'm not that crazy about eating them and I need nice-size trout for my work. It's unfortunate that many modern fly fishers return fish, and fish only barbless, for lofty reasons. Catching a fish and eating it is natural. Harassing

Releasing trout keeps a stream's equilibrium intact, and ensures that there will be good fishing for the next angler.

them solely for our own amusement might be construed as selfish (interesting word, huh—sel-fish?). No doubt fish prefer torture over death, but personally I see no high moral ground onto which we catch-and-release anglers should climb.

Handle with Care

If you are planning to release a trout, never put your fingers in its gills or lift it by hooking a finger under the gill plates. Instead, hold trout, especially large ones, horizontally and upside down when they are out of the water. Not only does that position decrease their struggling, but it is also easier on their internal organs, which aren't used to gravity the way we are.

To ensure that fish can be released in healthy condition, always play them for as short a time as possible. Therefore, use the heaviest tippet with which you can get away. Trout caught in warmwater lakes are much more susceptible to death from fishing than those caught in moving water. River fish can nose up to white water to get oxygen, often in great concentrations, but stillwater fish aren't so fortunate. If a fish shows signs of succumbing, put it back in the water immediately and resuscitate it.

Trout Revival

Always revive a fish in calm water by placing one finger in its mouth and pulling the fish back and forth slowly. Most people do this much too fast. Make the length of the stroke about equal to the length of the fish. Some fish may go into shock when released, especially in warm water, so release a weakened fish where it can be watched and recovered, in shallow water. Then, if it turns belly-up, you can retrieve it and attempt to revive it. If deep water prevents you from aiding a sick trout, try gently nudging it with your rod. This prodding is sometimes enough to bring it out of shock.

I have noticed that most anglers don't know when they should revive a fish, and often fool around with them unnecessarily.

Artificial respiration is very seldom needed for trout being returned to fast, cold water. The released fish may appear a bit faint at first, but a few tumbles down the current will bring it around.

Hook Removal

When folks have a hard time getting the hook out of the fish, it is usually because they are holding the fly too close to the hook eye and the hook merely pivots, or rocks, back and forth. Whether you use forceps or fingers, you need to grasp the hook at the very end of the shank, right above the bend. From that position it can be pushed straight back. Pushing it out is easier to do, of course, if the hook has been debarbed.

I find that a catch-and-release tool works very well on small trout, that is, fish light enough to be lifted up by the leader. Apply the tool to the leader with your free hand anywhere above the fish, run it down onto the fly, give a little twist, and no more trout. By using the tool, you don't have to touch the fish or fly, saving wear and tear on both. The tool is far less useful for releasing larger fish because it needs to be applied to a snug leader, and if a hefty fish is hanging on the leader, it will break.

Blood Needn't Signal Fatal Injury

I used to think that all trout bleeding from the gills were bound to die and should be harvested, but recently, while fishing in a beaver pond, I caught a very large brown that was bleeding badly from the gills. No way was I interested in lugging this 5-pound fish around, so I worked like an emergency-room doctor to revive it. And by God, in a few minutes the bleeding had stopped. I released the fish, and it was swimming around in the pond the following day. I don't know if the large size and vigorous health of the trout saved it, but since that experience I don't keep many wounded fish.

Hold the fish out of water briefly, take photos quickly, then get it back into the water.

Photos Should Be Snap Shots

When taking photos of a fish that you plan to return to the water be sure to make it snappy. Hold the fish out of the water for only very brief periods, or take your photos with the fish halfway in the water so that it is breathing water rather than air. Recent studies have shown that this is a prime factor in survival rates.

Chapter 27

EXPLORING FOR TROUT

I live and guide close to one of the country's most popular fishing holes, New Mexico's San Juan River. I also spend a lot of time fishing the wild waters of Patagonia, Argentina. Even there, at the other end of the world, I am often asked about the fishing on the San Juan. The sound of big fish splashing carries a long way. When I tell the Argentine fly fisherman that it is too crowded for my tastes and that I haven't fished it in years, they say. "Just where do you fish in that desert, if you don't fish there?" There are plenty of other places to fish. I even wrote a book on the subject—albeit a thin one. You just have to look.

Herd mentality and the allure of big fish send 90 percent of fly fishermen to the 10 percent of water that everyone hears so much about. It's like a popular restaurant in my hometown. Most locals think the food is okay, but inferior to a lot of other nearby restaurants. To the tourist, however, it's the living end. "Someone back in Witherspoon told us," they say, "'You have to eat at Harvey's.'" There is always a line to get in the place. It's the same with trout fishing spots: Those that everyone knows about may be good, but that doesn't mean there isn't someplace else to go that's as good or better—perhaps even a place without a waiting line.

Those popular big tailwaters are fabulous. You can catch big fish, have fun, and learn a lot at the same time. One good day on a river like the San Juan can teach you much about fighting large trout. Also, such waters are great for people with little time because the trails to such places are well worn and easy to follow.

One of the true joys of fishing is finding a new spot. Solitude, beautiful surroundings, good fishing: What more could you possible want?

You'll know in advance what fly to fish in which fashion. Remember, however, that most of these heavily fished places will have neurotic trout that will be selective and need to be fished for in a singular fashion. A guide, at least for your first day, is highly recommended.

But I like being alone, and I relish finding and fishing new water. I get tired of civilized places and want a little adventure, exercise, and solitude with my fishing. The good news is that plenty of those places exist. The bad news is that the trails to these spots are faint and poorly marked. Of course, if you love wild trout and the places in which they thrive, that's good news.

Ask Questions First

Presume that no matter how remote a place seems, someone knows more about it than you do. I spent a lot of time exploring blue holes, chasing bonefish and snapper with my son Nick in the vast and remote interior of South Andros Island in the

Bahamas. We'd go so far back in the bush, we'd say, "We must be the first men to ever fish this place." It was like being the modern Lewis and Clark of fly fishing. Later, when we talked the place up to someone in our confidence, he'd say, "Oh yeah, mon, you mean where dat bush en' little blue hole is, wid all dem snappar."

Instead of wandering around blindly to find the place, we could have asked first and perhaps headed there in a much straighter line. We fisherfolk, however, seem to have an inordinate amount of pride. It's tough to swallow that lump and ask questions. It's like rolling down the window in a strange town and asking directions; sometimes they're wrong, but more often they are right on. Of course, getting directions to Wal-Mart is considerably easier than getting directions to somebody's honey hole, especially if the bearer of the information has nothing more to gain than seeing your ugly face at his favorite spot. Don't be surprised to hear that it's a long drive, a miserable hike, and that rattlesnakes await your arrival. One of the best places I've ever fished had ingenious signs warning of radioactivity, obviously erected by some clever angler. At least, I hope that's the case and that the ringing in my ears is from too much espresso.

Be warned, however, to consider the consequences before you ask certain people to show you their secret fishing spots. I have a couple of good fishing holes for which I sold my soul, vowing, "No, I won't take anyone, no not even my children, here." So I'm lonely when I fish there. On occasion it can be better to go the extra distance and find such secrets on your own rather than be in debt the rest of you life.

Fly shops have good information, but it's of great value to them. Tight-lipped shopkeepers may irritate fly fishermen, but try putting yourself in their shoes, and maybe you'll understand their position. Remember that what's a passionate pastime to you is a living to them. Some guy who may be a cutthroat businessman at home arrives on the fishing scene and expects "free love" at water's edge. Not much is free these days, and I can tell you as a former fly-shop owner that the value of the information will generally rise with the value of goods purchased. Of course, everyone everywhere is different, and you might just walk into a shop and be given the map to old Walter's hideout.

Where fishing pressure is not an issue, free love may still be practiced. This unfortunately leaves out most of the continental United States.

Get a Guide

A good fly-fishing guide will take you to places that he knows well, places where the results are predictable. If you are looking for someplace wild and unfished, you might ask the guide if there is somewhere he has been meaning to explore, and say that you would be willing to participate in the experiment. I love that kind of job because there is always someplace, or some stretch of a familiar river, that I want to check out but haven't. Of course, if I'm getting paid to go, that's fantastic. The client will be taking a gamble but will get to see how the guide goes about the exploration. Because he's bought a partnership for the day, he gets to share in the discovery.

Government Sources of Information

Government agencies—game and fish departments and Bureau of Land Management and Forest Service offices—can be excellent sources of information. Call them, as you should a fly shop, prior to your trip. When I had my fly shop, I was amazed that people would drive 1,000 miles, walk in the door and ask, "How's the fishing?" It's not always good, and it is best to know that before you pack the car.

The government offices will have maps, regulations, and current road, weather, and water conditions. More importantly, they have fisheries biologists on staff who are, surprisingly, seldom quizzed by the public. Often, these biologists don't fish for sport, so they will unhesitatingly tell you the truth. A fisheries biologist once told me about a nest of huge brown trout he had found.

"Yes, 3-pound brown trout are in a beaver pond up there," he said in a matter-of-fact manner, "but you have to walk a quarter mile and cross two fences to get to them." He just as well could have been telling me that he had found a rare subspecies of termite. Game wardens, too, can be a great source of information, being out in the field every day. Most view part of their job as helping people get their fish and game and are usually more than happy to be of service.

Treasures Close to Home

For those who live in congested areas, don't despair; good fishing may be closer—much closer—than you might think. Instead of looking for what would appear to be the choice sections of a creek, you may want to head the other way. Many of the best fishing—and hunting—places that I have found are ones that are simply overlooked because everyone assumes that they are overused. Even in the West, the best water can often be found where you would least expect it to be—next to houses, dumps, thrift stores, and other detractions from the natural landscape. Let me put it this way: If there are two sections of an accessible stream, one idyllic, the other running by a gravel pit and under a stack of junk cars, try the dumpy spot.

If you are in the habit of driving by a piece of river or stream often, notice which sections get fished and how much pressure they seem to be receiving. Certain areas will receive much less pressure than others will. Perhaps the lack of parking areas or the presence of an unchained malamute keeps pressure down on a promising stretch of stream. Figure out how to access and fish some sweet little spot. Slide in and out of it like a thief in the night, using whatever it takes—disguises, lies, you name it. All's fair in love, war—and the whisper of fishing spots.

Explore Times as Well as Places

When planning trips to places where fishing pressure is an issue, it can be wise to fish weekdays and times when others don't. Some of the best fishing in the West can be in the pre-runoff in early spring. That's when the fish are starving, the trees are greening, and the caddis are hatching—but the anglers are still in hibernation!

Know What You're Looking For

It is always nice to know what resides in the water you plan to fish. You can sometimes get fish-per-mile statistics from fly shops, fisheries biologists, or fishing friends. For the kind of wild water for which you may be looking, however, those numbers are probably unavailable. You will have to figure that out on your own.

I always feel excited when I step into new water, especially when that step coincides with the dining schedule of the stream's residents. I feel blessed then, because from that feeding period I will have a fairly clear picture of the river's fish population. They don't even need to eat for very long. If they feed actively in one pool, I can guesstimate what is swimming around in the next one, because if the next pool is similar to the one from which you caught fish, it should hold an equal number of trout. Obviously, the better you can read water the more accurate the count will be. This research work is an advanced form of angling that is beyond catch and release. You get to count the fish you caught, the ones you missed, and even those you just saw; they all go into the equation.

Get an Overview

I always try to see as much of a stream as I can on my first visit. That way I will know where the best water is for future trips. I'll do this by keeping an eye out for trout while walking briskly along the bank. If the fish are at all active, you should get to see quite a few of the rascals before they can dodge you. If you don't see any fish, don't despair. That doesn't mean there aren't any. It may simply mean that they aren't feeding and are lying up.

My favorite method of exploring a new stream is to use a combination of the aforementioned techniques. By fishing only the best holes and walking over the rest of the water, I not only get the exploring job done, but also hopefully get to catch some nice trout while doing it.

If Big Fish Are the Objective

Seemingly, the best places to fish are those with a high number of trout, but that is not always the case. Some of my favorite rivers don't hold many fish, but the trout are big. The low fish count keeps the fishing pressure down, because when the average guy fishes it, he really doesn't know exactly where to fish and goes home skunked, never to return. We guides love that kind of stream because those lonely big fish are seldom bothered and may be gullible. If you fished only the places capable of holding big trout, you could have some very good sport.

Big fish like this feed for short spells, then turn off. Catching them means fishing when conditions are ideal.

Large trout, however, are efficient diners and seldom eat for long spells, especially when they have plenty of space and food. To catch the fish on the feed you either need to do a lot of fishing until you hit the right time or know when conditions are perfect. The latter may be a combination of favorable water levels and temperatures, combined with the availability of big bugs like stoneflies or hoppers. Obviously this second choice beats the hell out the first option of possible hours of fruitless fishing, so find out all you can. When everything looks right, go for it.

Where Fish Are Plentiful

At the other end of the scale, when fish numbers are so high that they push the carrying capacity of their environment, the fish will have to feed a lot. This is often carried to the extreme on streams where nonnative species have been introduced, because they seem to overpopulate more than the indigenous fish do.

This is the case with most rivers in the U.S., spawning a new, ever-growing push to reestablish native species. Though this movement is well intentioned, much of the natives' home water is too silted and warm for them now. To fill that rather large slot, we are very fortunate to have the tougher nonnative trout.

Populations Are Dynamic

The composition of a stream is dynamic, that is, always changing. It is possible to see the size, number, and even species change over time. One stream that I know of in Colorado used to swarm with small brook trout, but now, ten years later, it is inhabited solely by good-size browns.

Environmental Factors Affect Trout

Logging, grazing, development, and irrigation are important things to consider when sizing up new water. Learning to understand what roles these factors play in your fishing will put you one rung up on the ladder toward being an expert angler and outdoorsman and serve you well in your pursuit of productive trout waters.

•*Irrigation.* It's June in the Rockies—heaven on earth—and you wade into a gorgeous piece of water that winds through rich, green farmland. Flycatchers flit out of the streamside alders to grab mayflies. The world is alive with life, and the fishing is good. The memory of the fishing and the beautiful river visit your waking and sleeping thoughts often over the next couple of months, but when you finally return you find not that lovely, healthy river, but a skinny trickle of water that has been shrunk by thirsty farms.

When river levels drop like that, fish may head for cooler water above irrigation head gates or hunker down in the few remaining deep holes. The larger browns will hide under banks, roots, and trees. Those fish are virtually uncatchable in summer's low and warm water—during the daytime. They are, however, very catchable if you linger late into the evening. By "late," I mean when stars flicker in the sky and you need a flashlight to get back to the car.

When fishing such low water, hightail it from one hole to the next. Unlike higher water, when the fish can be anywhere, the low flow means that you will at least know where they are. This low-water problem will be exacerbated if there is considerable grazing along the river.

•*Grazing* is a huge factor, especially on smaller creeks in the West. I know of one stream with incredible trout numbers in its rocky, canyon stretch, because the boulders aren't affected by the cattle's hooves and appetite. When the stream emerges from the canyon and heads into flat meadowlands, the trout population plummets. This is where the lazy bovine whiles away the day, all his needs met at streamside. He munches the bright green grass on the bank and then, with a simple 180-degree maneuver, turns and hurls the brown remains into the river. Alas, this isn't even the cow's worst contribution. That "honor" belongs to its huge round hooves as they flatten and trample the streambank. Their munching and mashing of riparian vegetation drastically reduces the lush growth, causing terrestrial and aquatic insects to lose their homes and water temperatures to rise due to lack of shade. In warmer climes that are on the brink of modern trout range, such as the Gila wilderness in southwestern New Mexico, you will not find trout in streams where substantial grazing occurs.

On the bright side, more and more streams on both public and private land are being fenced to avoid this desecration. Ranchers are finding it in their best interest, because when the area adjacent to the stream is fenced, the water table is higher, which is important in dry times.

Just as in places that are overgrazed, the defoliation of a watershed will cause the waters to rise and fall drastically. In an area with which I am familiar only a couple of streams have never been logged or grazed. This, of course, not only makes them solid trout streams, but also allows them to be studied in comparisons with the more average, abused watersheds. The most glaring contrast can be seen during runoff, when the logged streams are over their banks with brown water, while the pristine watersheds run full but clear. Because the pristine creeks are not grazed, the root structure of the native plants holds the banks together. The banks of the abused creeks crumble, washing downriver with each flood.

The healthy stream's runoff will last well into summer and maintain a good flow until snowfall. When I hear about another horrible flood somewhere, I am always amazed that the reasons why these catastrophes are constantly happening are so seldom mentioned.

Mines Matter

Contrary to what spokesmen for mining operations might say, I believe that their influence has never been of any particular benefit to any watershed. I'm especially touchy on this subject, having lived through the demise of what was probably the richest trout stream that I have ever fished, the Red River in northern New Mexico. Twenty years ago this incredible little river regularly produced wild cuttbows of 3 and 4 pounds. Large-scale mining of molybdenum, by Unocal of California, killed those fish—and they have yet to return.

Guidebooks

A lot of fishing guidebooks cover various states and regions. Those that aren't very wordy are probably of more value afield than the thicker models. These guides can be of great help, but as the author of one I can safely say that you won't find everything you need to know in them. When reading guidebooks or magazine articles, keep in mind that not everything can be revealed. I remember that when I wrote my guidebook I struggled over whether to include a number of places. I wanted to be both responsible to the place and to the reader as well. Certainly you don't want to ruin water by drawing too much attention to it. I had learned this lesson the hard way when I wrote about a sweet little spot in another guidebook some years ago. That book became popular, and that no doubt contributed to the considerable increase in fishing pressure on that once peaceful stream. Also bear in mind that some spots are unknown to the writer; others are too delicate and small to reveal; and yet others are spoken of only in whispers.

Do Homework for Lake Exploration

In exploring lakes, place considerable emphasis on homework. Because most trout lakes in the West don't support natural reproduction and, instead, rely on stocking, much can be learned from fisheries biologists. Ask about winterkill and food. Many high-elevation lakes serve trout only skimpy meals—midges and terrestrials. If, however, you learn that there are freshwater shrimp and/or snails, grab your rod because fish get big on that grub.

Field Work

Let's get outside where a fisherman is supposed to be. We'll be armed, of course, with the proper research equipment—waders, rods, flies, and so on.

I write this overlooking the Quilquihue River in Argentina. I'm again involved in the painstaking work of finding good fishing for my clients. Just below my window the fish are small, but I'm hoping that with a hike downriver, and away from the road, I'll find fish that grow larger.

I walk some 40 dusty minutes and slide down the steep bank and wade out into the river. I go ahead and cast indiscriminately in some fast water because I believe there will be monsters everywhere. I do catch a small rainbow, but he's not what I had in mind. So I go upstream in search of better water. This river is new to me, so I should only be fishing water in which I have confidence. The water and the sky are both very clear, so I'll fish fast and only at the heads of the pools. The fish will be easier to fool there, and that is usually where the feeding fish will be. I will fish only these really good spots because, after all, I've got a lot of river to myself.

I may walk half a mile and make only a few casts, but I might also stand in one spot and throw a hundred times. Knowing how many casts to put in a place according to the quality of that spot is the secret here. Having taught a number of individuals to fly-fish, I have seen how the learning process works for trout fishermen. In a few seasons a person will learn to cast, hook, and play fish. He or she will, at the same time, gain some knowledge of insects and flies. The last, most difficult and most important part of the training, learning to read water, takes a lifetime of study.

In doing this scouting I pay great attention to sign on the banks. Is there a trail, and is it well used? If there are many footprints, I hope they are tracks of felt soles, because that would indicate catch-and-release fishermen. I come across a most gruesome find, a recent camp where fish have been grilled

A hidden jewel in the southern Rockies. Scouting, indeed, can pay off.

on a spit. That's like finding the fox's track on the way into the henhouse.

When's Dinner?

I also investigate streamside how much food is available and at what time of year or day a particular place will fish best. The food factor is fairly simple. I look under the rocks out from the water's edge and note the insects and their abundance. If I find a lot of stonefly nymphs, I'll be there in early summer for the hatch. If I am looking in the spring and see grass starting to grow streamside, I know that I may have fishing on hoppers later in the summer.

What time of day will the particular body of water fish best? Streams that flow west may fish best late in the day, when the sun is at your back. This is especially true on a small stream where trout tend to be wild and spooky. Such fish can see you coming from a long ways off if they have the sun in their favor. Whenever possi-

A fat brown, from a secret spot. Sometimes it pays to keep that spot a closely guarded secret.

ble, in any fishing situation, it is wise to have the sun behind you. You will have a better view of the fish, your fly, and the bottom.

A Final Hint

When you find that dream spot where big trout lazily drift up to inhale dry flies, the tough part is not bragging about it. From considerable and painful experience I can assure you that it won't be as important a secret to the next person you tell. Its confidentiality becomes less and less honored as it gets blabbed about down the line, and before you know it the place will be overrun. You'll hate yourself for ever opening your mouth to anyone about it. If you have to brag, do what I do: Finish your story with a lie.

Chapter 28

MAPS

You can learn a lot about proposed fishing spots by studying maps. If you are looking for out-of-the-way water, start your search with state highway maps. Here you can get the big picture, which may be far more important than you might think. Because the kind of water we're looking for is probably not close to any big cities, slide your finger across the highway map until it settles where the roads turn thin and wavy. Then, when you know the general area you want to fish, switch to government maps. Forest Service or Bureau of Land Management maps don't give you the lay of the land, that is, the topography, but they will reveal land ownership. This avoids the embarrassing situation of hiking 20 miles only to have Ted Turner throw you off one of his ranches.

Topographic maps are the final step. They can be found at bookstores, outdoor stores, and surveying offices. They can be purchased from afar by writing to Map Branch of Distribution, U.S. Geological Survey, Box 25286, M.S.-306, Denver, CO 80225. For information, you can call 303-202-4700. If you are doing your trout studies by computer, visit www.usgs.gov. Another excellent Web site is www.mapquest.com.

Besides revealing the roads, trails, and topography, careful study can tell you much more. For instance, in small mountain streams, the flatter, open areas are where large beaver dams might be found. If you take that one step further, look for nearby springs or very small tributaries. Dams in main channels generally wash out during runoff, but the dams on smaller feeder creeks and springs may stay intact for years, long enough to grow large trout.

In beaver country you never know when the investigation into such little brooks will pay off. Last year I spied one creek that looked especially promising because it had plant life. Aquatic plants, especially watercress, may signify that the stream is spring fed, and spring creeks are very rich. I hiked up the foot-wide creek for about a mile until I came to the Hoover Dam of beaver dams. It closed off a small canyon and stood about 15 feet high. The aspen logs that comprised the dam were all old and gray, so I knew that the dam had been there long enough to grow big fish. The spring poured out of the earth just above the pond, giving it a rich and stable water supply, unaffected by the floods of the nearby river. I ascended a little hill to have a look down into the pond. From this height I could see into the clear water perfectly and saw what was to become the biggest trout that I have ever caught in the U.S. It actually took me three years to

Careful map study can help you find underfished areas that may hold monsters like this.

catch Wally, as I came to call him, but the story of his capture could be another book in itself.

Whether checking maps of large or small rivers, pay attention to the "snakier" sections because the winding of the stream creates deep pools. Also look for areas where tributaries and side canyons join a river as they add character, in the form of boulders, rocks, and wood, to the main flow.

Another feature of topo maps is that they reveal whether you are looking at meadow or forest. Open areas are white, and timbered country is green. This can be of help in the hunt for user-friendly high lakes to fish in the West. Bring a lot of flies to the lakes surrounded with green because the trees will probably end up wearing many of them. Besides looking for treeless banks to fish, also look for level shorelines where the contour lines are far apart, because those shores will probably ease off into the shallow, wadable water that feeding fish like. Contrary to popular belief, on lake and stream, the shallower water produces the most life—and best fishing.

If your interest lies in finding the most remote and least fished water, study topo maps for areas that lie beyond canyon walls, mountains, and other nuisances. Always bear in mind two things: People love to catch and eat fish; but people are basically lazy and the amount of fishing pressure that a particular piece of water gets is usually in direct proportion to the effort required in getting there.

But that statement needs to be qualified: Twenty years ago if you hiked a distance into the backcountry, you could be fairly sure you would be alone. Today, however, some areas of the U.S. are filled with vigorous people who think nothing of hiking five miles for a day's fishing. So if you are headed up a trail, and what looks like the Olympic cross-country fly-fishing team sweeps past you, don't hesitate to change your plans and fish closer to the car. In some places, you may actually find less fishing pressure there than at the end of the trail.

Chapter 29

YOU SHOULD HAVE BEEN HERE YESTERDAY

If all of the little tricks in this book fail you, here is my final advice.

I'm a professional in the fly-fishing business. That means that, like every professional, I know what to do when things aren't going well: Make up an excuse. I have spent considerable time exploring the evasive world of the fishing excuse, and not being able to continually repeat just one, I have had to develop many.

The Tried-and-True Excuse

First, make the most use out of the tried-and-true "You should have been here yesterday." It is hard to beat because it proclaims, "Yes there are fish in the river," and "You are close to having caught them." Be sure to find out if the inquirer had actually fished yesterday. If he or she had, then "You should have been here yesterday" obviously needs expansion to "You should have been here last week," or "month" or "year," depending on the time of his last outing.

Blame It on Mother Nature

When designing a proper excuse, remember to draw attention away from yourself. You can't say, "I can't fish very well, so I did-n't catch any." No, you have to insert "because." It's because "the moon was full" or "there was no moon." "The water was too muddy" or it was "too clear." The water (or the air temperature) was "too warm," or "too cold." "The air was too windy," or "too still." "The weather was too rainy," or "too dry." You don't have to look far for an intelligent-sounding excuse. The whole natural world is waiting to be at fault, and best of all, it can't talk back.

Don't Paint Yourself into a Corner

You have to be careful, however, not to paint yourself into a corner. I learned that as a kid on one of my first guiding jobs. I had no idea how to catch fish in the lake at which we found ourselves, so I needed to point an accusing finger somewhere. You'd think I would have been safe finding fault with wind direction with four from which to choose. A convenient east wind made me look good at the start, for everyone knows, "When the wind is out of the east, the fishing is the least." This worked for a while, but it was a swirly sort of day. Still, thinking that the breeze would never do a 180, I unfortunately muttered, "When the wind is from the west, the fishing is the best." When the dreaded west wind arrived, I rowed in circles attempting to disorient the client.

The One-Word Reply

At least other fishermen have sympathy to bad luck because we've all been there. The person who doesn't fish is a tougher sell. I particularly dread encounters with rafters. These idlers already have an attitude against us because they don't know how to fish and just aimlessly float down the river. Between the brief moments of exhilaration that the rapids provide they search for a hapless angler to molest. They travel in loose packs, with each boat spaced just far enough apart so that each group gets to ask, "How they bitin'?" The brief conversation is reiterated to each gang, and if you've caught some fish, you don't mind the question. You might even welcome it. If, however, you haven't had any success, answering in the negative over and over again is ego deflating. If the water is running fast, they sail by mercifully quickly, but an elaborate excuse is then impossible, and you are reduced to a brief "yes" or "no" answer. What is needed here is some sort of stylish, one-word comeback. I heard one in the Caribbean a few years ago that has the proper attitude. While walking by an old Bahamian gentleman who was sleepily sitting over his "trow line," I gave him the old "Are they biting?" Without breaking his restful stride, he replied, "Presently."

The fly fisherman, with his endless theories, tiny flies, and skinny leaders, has a bottomless pool of excuses. Fly fishing is an equal-opportunity sport where the not-so-talented can make up for catching by the accumulation of knowledge. This information may help catch a fish from time to time, but its real use is in the crafting of the clever fishing excuse. Failure can be turned into relative success by adopting a pensive air and saying, "I knew that they were taking No. 22 spent tricos and I to go with a 7X tippet. But although I played the creature with impunity it was just too fine a leader and the bloody fish broke me off…"

Catch and Release Opens New Opportunities

Catch-and-release fishing allows the unlucky angler even greater victories and puts us in a place where excuse isn't even needed. That place lies just beyond a bend in the river, out of sight from your fishing partner. You are now free to say, "I knew that they were taking No. 22 spent tricos and that I would have to go with a 7X tippet—I played the monster with impunity and released the brute unscathed."

Another tactic is to bypass or rise above mere fishing. Shift your priorities a little to accommodate the situation. For instance, a poor day on the water can handily be turned into a great picnic. "Fish? Yeah, I think we caught some. Hell, I forget. It was such a nice day in that beautiful place—and that lunch!" Or you can transcend such earthly pursuits and rise to a spiritual level higher than a dry-fly purist. Quote something from Jung, like "I ply the depths of my soul when I fish." Who's going to hassle you when you hand out that kind of jive?

I just guided a North American businessman in Argentina

who had one week to catch all the fishes in Patagonia. On his last day he pounded the water like Rambo on a rampage, in the face of one of the best fishing excuses known—a windy cold front. When he finally gave up he was too depressed for me to humor him with any of my flippant lines. He didn't say a thing all the way back to town, and that gave me time to reflect on how important catch-and-release fly fishing really is.

While Rambo sulked, my line of thinking directed me to a new tactic. This season, when I get pestered about the quality of the fishing, I'm going to say, "Fishing! People are eating rocks and sticks, our country resembles ancient Rome before the fall, dogs are sleeping with cats, and lawyers openly high-five each other. The world is a crumbling, stumbling wreck, and you want to talk about a fish."

If you hear me say something like that, you can bet the fishing sucked, and, yes, "You should have been here yesterday."

Fish with Taylor Streit

Taylor Streit runs a guiding business out of Taos, New Mexico. Fishing the Rio Grande, San Juan, and many other streams in both New Mexico and southern Colorado, his staff of guides teaches fly fishing and casting while on the water. Their intuitive style of instruction takes the mystery out of what may appear to be a complicated sport.

In the winter months Taylor and his son, Nick, take anglers to Patagonia, Argentina. These trips are customized to each group's needs and arranged so that the clients experience the unique Argentine lifestyle.

Streit does clinics and seminars and often speaks for fly-fishing clubs. He also conducts schools for all levels of fly fishers, based on "Instinctive Fly Fishing." He can be reached at www.streitfly-fishing.com or phoned at (505) 751–1312.

Index

Page numbers in boldface refer to photographs